CITIZEN ACTION
AND THE
NEW AMERICAN
POPULISM

CITIZEN ACTION
AND THE
NEW AMERICAN
POPULISM

HARRY C. BOYTE, HEATHER BOOTH,

AND STEVE MAX

Temple University Press
Philadelphia

Temple University Press, Philadelphia 19122

Copyright © 1986 by Temple University

All rights reserved

Published 1986

Printed in the United States of America

The paper used in this publication meets
the minimum requirements of
American National Standards for
Information Sciences—Permanence of
Paper for Printed Library Materials.

ANSI Z39.48-1984

Library of Congress Cataloging-in-Publication Data

Boyte, Harry Chatten, 1945–

Citizen action.

Bibliography: p.

Includes index.

1. Political participation—United States.
2. Citizens' associations—United States. 3. Populism—
United States. 4. United States—Politics and government—1981– . I. Booth, Heather, 1950– .
II. Max, Steve. III. Title.

JK1764.B69   1986   323′.042′0973   86-5786

ISBN 0-87722-424-2 (alk. paper)

CONTENTS

ACKNOWLEDGMENTS

A work like this is, necessarily, a collegial undertaking. We think of this book as a beginning statement about the new progressive populism, which we hope will spark wide ranging, lively discussion. This is also an effort that seeks to express the distinctive perspectives of an emerging social force, a fledgling movement. These perspectives grow out of the experiences and stories of many people in recent years who fought for their communities, and who have thought about the broader meanings and lessons of their struggles.

The particular views expressed here are, in the final analysis, ones for which we alone take responsibility. However, we have benefitted immensely from careful readings, specific discussions, and, in several cases, direct contributions to this work. Don Wiener, Alice Palmer, Allan Dreyer, Jackie Kendall, Michael Ansara, Ira Arlook, Bob Hudek, and David Blakenhorn gave us invaluable feedback and suggestions about the shape of the overall argument. Ansara and Wiener collaborated in some of the writing. Mike Podhorzer, Ed Rothschild, John O'Connor, Barbara Helmick, and Larry Marx offered numerous detailed suggestions about sections of the work.

Gail Siegel, Carol Browner, Robert Creamer, Becky Glass, and Peter Handler and Si Kahn made a number of helpful contributions along the way.

Many others have aided in typing sections of the manuscript, in collecting and sending information, and in other ways. This includes Sheryl Woodards and Patty Stroman. We wish to thank particularly our editors at Temple, Michael Ames and Doris Braendel, for their encouragement, suggestions, and unflagging efforts, often in the face of unexpected complications and delays. We also thank Ed Royce for helpful comments.

We also each have several personal acknowledgments we wish to mention. Harry Boyte appreciates discussions with Allan Isaacman, Tom Dewar, and, most especially, Sara Evans which were of great help in this work, as in earlier book projects.

Heather Booth gives grateful appreciation to her co-workers and allies, for their shared commitment and friendships, to her parents— Hazel and Jerry Tobis—for their rooting her world in a sense of values, to her children—Gene and Dan—who were her rock and give her hope, and to her husband—Paul—whose support and common vision made this work all the more possible and all the more worthwhile.

Steve Max thanks those who contributed materially and spiritually to the completion of this project: Kimberly Max, his daughter, whose favorite video movie is *Robin Hood*, and Lynn Peterson Max, his wife; Ellen Max, his mother; and Jackie Kendall, his boss and director of the Midwest Academy.

More broadly, we wish to express our deep appreciation for the thousands, even tens of thousands of citizen leaders, organizers, and activists —some known widely, most known only in their communities—from whom we have drawn inspiration. They embody the finest traditions of American democracy. This is their story. And to them we dedicate this work.

FOREWORD
by U.S. Senator Tom Harkin

I t has become fashionable these days to lament the passing of the age of idealism and commitment that spawned the civil rights, anti-Vietnam war, environmental, and arms control movements. Newsmagazines inform us we are now in the "Age of the Yuppie." Commitment has been replaced by cynicism, compassion by conspicuous consumption.

However, if journalism is—as was once noted—the first draft of history, I think the historians of a later age will write that the death knell of progressive political activism was sounded prematurely.

What happened to these democratic idealists? Did they give up or "sell out"? Some may have. But many just refocused their energies closer to home, organizing their neighbors to fight for such issues as better housing, fair taxation, lower utility rates, and the cleanup of toxic wastes. In many instances, they achieved spectacular success.

All over the country, ordinary citizens in the city and on the farm were making local government and businesses more responsive and accountable.

But this book, while chronicling their achievements, would not have been written if it had stopped there. *Citizen Action and the New American Populism* is about how these local efforts—thousands of disconnected universes—have been brought together to form a national network for progressive action.

Cutting across racial and class and geographical boundaries, these actions have shown millions of people that their common interests far outweigh their differences. To the farmers being forced off their land, the steelworker laid off his job, the senior citizen unable to pay winter heating bills, or the mother whose family's health is threatened by a nearby toxic waste dump, the message of citizen action is the same: Don't get mad, don't get frustrated, don't give up. Organize and fight back.

Political strategists of all stripes are realizing the latent power in this "populist" message. But the pseudo-populism of Ronald Reagan and Richard Viguerie is a divisive philosophy based on fear and insecurity and racism. Real democratic populism unites rather than divides, by giving people hope and power to put government back in their hands.

Real populism recognizes that the biggest problem in America is that too few people hold too much economic and political power. The stakes in the battle to redress this imbalance are extremely high. As the late Supreme Court Justice Louis Brandeis once said: "We can either have democracy in this country or we can have great wealth concentrated in the hands of a few, but we can't have both."

Progressive populism is no pie-in-the-sky ideology. It's practical politics that works and has broad-based appeal. I speak from experience. Citizen Action and other grass roots organizations played a key role in my election to the United States Senate in 1984.

No, the fight for social and economic justice has not died. Forged in the cauldron of Reaganomics, strengthened through shared adversity, and united by a common vision of America that lives up to its promise of equality and opportunity, it has re-emerged stronger than ever.

CITIZEN ACTION
AND THE
NEW AMERICAN
POPULISM

PRELUDE

---

estled in the foothills of the Ozarks, Castlewood had once seemed an ideal place to live. It was quiet, safe, a reminder of America's small town roots. During the long, hot, slow summer days, dust had drifted in the air, until the oil truck sprayed the roads. "The dioxin is all around this town," explained Robert Bagley, a local resident. "No one ever told us that the same spray truck was also used to haul dioxin. Now we're paying the price. Our health is threatened, but we can't get out of this place because who'd we ever sell our homes to? That's why we've got to send a message to Congress."[1]

The message was graphic. Photographers snapped pictures of the abandoned grocery store in Castlewood, emblazoned with a crudely painted skull and crossbones.

During September of 1985, from the four corners of the nation, trucks thundered down the interstate highways toward Washington. Often the trucks turned off on sideroads, attracting crowds of reporters to otherwise forgotten towns like Castlewood. At each stop along the way, local citizens loaded the trucks with evidence of the nation's toxic waste crisis.

It was called Superdrive for Superfund, an organizing and media campaign that climaxed more than a year of grass roots action across the country in support of strengthening the federal cleanup program called Superfund. Other communities sent messages with the trucks. At the Stringfellow Acid Pit in Glen Haven, California, fifty school children added their colored drawings of the ways in which the cancer causing trichlorethylene had changed their lives. In East Gray, Maine, Cathy Hinds sent the truck off with soil samples from the home she had lived in when her infant son had died from chemical exposure. Kathy Pittman of Holbrook, Massachusetts, included the wig worn by her mother when she lost her hair from cancer treatments made necessary by the toxics in her neighborhood. Along with the evidence, moreover, came a demonstration of grass roots citizen power. More than one million signatures, collected by door to door canvassers and citizen organizations, demanded that Congress take effective action to do something about the crisis of toxic waste.

The four trucks met in Washington, after stopping in 120 American communities. Some members of Congress at first balked at the idea of receiving such "pieces of their district" as toxic waste samples. But when reporters questioned them, almost all reversed their opinions. As politicians usually do, they were looking over their shoulders. Polls by Yankelovich, Skelly and White had found that 79 percent of the public believed "not enough" had been done to clean up toxic waste sites. A strong plurality believed that current laws did not go far enough. Sixty-three percent were convinced that those protections that existed were not being enforced strictly enough. On September 26, 1985, the day the trucks arrived in Washington, the U.S. Senate voted overwhelmingly to give the toxic cleanup program five times more money than it had budgeted in its original authorization.

Grass roots organizing had unmistakably made the difference. Since 1979, the chemical industry's political action committees—called PACs for short—have contributed $22 million to U.S. House and Senate candidates in an effort to weaken any federal legislation about toxic chemicals. In October, 1984, the Senate had voted 59 to 38 against allowing the Superfund reauthorization bill even to come to the floor for debate, though the program's initial authorization was running out. Those senators who had voted to prevent debate received an average contribution of $101,000 from chemical PACs. The issue had been taken out of Washington. Canvassers for citizen groups had reached more than twelve million households over the subsequent year. Candidates for Senate like Paul Simon, an advocate of strong federal action, had won against incumbent Republicans who sided with industry, even in the midst of the Reagan landslide. All told, it was a case of "the people being heard," in a political climate where, to jaded and supposedly sophisticated observers, the idea of grass roots democracy seemed often simply quaint.[2]

Superfund was not the only issue where progressive citizen lobbying had paid off in the Reagan years. Despite enormous contributions to congressional campaigns, the oil giants had been defeated year after year on their most sought-after prize, decontrol of natural gas. Industry was beaten as well on reauthorizations of the Clean Water Act and the Safe Drinking Water Act. When Reagan budget-cutters sought to take a knife to Social Security, Medicare, and Medicaid in 1985, hundreds of thousands of senior citizens and the poor met with politicians across the country and defeated the attempt.

At state and local levels, progressive citizen campaigns achieved even more successes. Farm activists won legislation to extend credit to family farmers. Utility customers blocked nuclear power plants, cut back utility cost overruns, and won direct election of utility commission members. Grass roots movements expanded educational programs, opened up government meetings to the public, forced companies to give notice—in some cases, compensation—if they planned to move, and won new jobs programs and aid for small businesses.

Such victories and the stories behind them are the subject of this book. *Citizen Action and the New American Populism* details especially the work of Citizen Action, one of the leading organizations in a progressive citizen movement that had begun to make itself felt even before the Reagan victory in 1980. Far from being the death knell for such activism, the political changes of the 1980s expanded and deepened citizen efforts and moved them toward a broader vision that begins to add up to far more than a series of issue campaigns.

Most broadly, that citizen movement is an alternative to feelings of despair and defeat that afflict many Americans in our times. It is the story about the importance and power of united grass roots efforts in an increasingly centralized society, about belief in human dignity and the sacredness of our planet. It indicates the re-emergence in modern America of our country's most ancient vision: the conviction that ours, properly, is a government of the people, by the people, and for the people, dedicated to liberty and justice for all.

1. THUNDER ON THE RIGHT

*In the last several years, Americans have literally stood by
and watched as godless, spineless leaders have brought our nation
floundering to the brink of death. . . . Middle class Americans tired of
Big Government, Big Business, Big Labor and Big Education telling us
what to do and what not to do . . . must make their feelings known. . . .
The vacuum of leadership in America must be filled.
Conservative Americans must now take the helm and guide
America back to a position of stability and greatness.*

Jerry Falwell, 1980

By the mid-1980s the Reagan revolution ousted from favor virtually
the whole consensus dominating American politics for the last fifty
years. That consensus had taken shape in the wake of the 1929 stock
market crash and the depression that followed. It said, in short, that because the forces of the free market had brought the country to economic
disaster and because the ensuing unemployment and poverty had mobilized millions of Americans, it was now up to the federal government to
step in and prevent each of these two things from ever happening again.
The half century that followed was marked by ongoing government
efforts to regulate the economy and by an expanding "Safety Net," protecting citizens from at least the most catastrophic consequences of the
failure of those efforts. With the election of Reagan, this consensus began to fall apart.

From the bitter experience of Vietnam, a new caution entered American foreign policy. It turned out that human rights did affect a government's claim on the loyalty of its people. Citizens questioned the ability and virtue of America's policing the world and intervening against regimes not to their liking. Politicians grudgingly acknowledged—if they did not always adhere to—the principle of self-determination. Most Americans came to recognize the danger of nuclear disaster and placed hope in the possibility of negotiated disarmament. With the election of Ronald Reagan, the nation's foreign policy leaders and military strategists began to abandon such caution.

From our earliest history as a colony of dissenters from the officially established religions of Europe came the strong constitutionally based principle of the separation of church and state. The state was not to use the power of religious doctrine to enforce the moral precepts of any particular religion. With Ronald Reagan's election, those who sought to impose their own religious convictions upon the entire nation took new heart and gained new recognition.

Other long cherished and hard won commitments have been set aside by the administration—the commitment to end race and sex discrimination, the commitment to the right of working people to organize unions and to share in the nation's growing wealth, the commitment to preserve the environment, and the commitment to make taxes fall most heavily on those with the greatest ability to pay.

Issues that had seemed settled once again turned into open debates. The attorney general challenged the ancient writ of habeas corpus, which since the Middle Ages had allowed appeal against unjust imprisonment. He questioned whether the Bill of Rights applies to the states, a matter resolved by the Civil War.

A decade before, political pundits would have scoffed at the thought of such gains by the right wing. Ronald Reagan was written off as an extremist from California. Observers proclaimed the Republican Party dead in the aftermath of Watergate and Richard Nixon's resignation. But a simple idea that seemed archaic and backward-looking from the point of view of many political commentators nonetheless had begun to resonate profoundly with ordinary citizens. That idea was expressed in many ways, but the typical sentiments from an employee of a tool and farm machinery store in North Carolina, Cameron Johnson, summed it up. "The common people don't have any representation anymore. Everybody's pretty well dissatisfied, but they don't know who to blame it on."

Ronald Reagan provided an answer. Power, he argued in 1976, had flowed toward the elite in government. "States and local communities," he proclaimed, had become "little more than . . . bureaucratic subdivisions of . . . government in Washington." The solution was also simple. "Reverse the flow of power," he said. "Return to the human scale that people can understand and cope with, the scale of the local fraternal lodge, the church organization, the block club, the farm bureau." [1]

The New Movements: Right Wing versus Progressive Populism

Ronald Reagan spoke for and was brought to power by a social movement that was much broader than the Republican Party. For almost two decades, through the 1960s and 1970s, a new breed of right wing activists had organized at the grass roots, speaking to a discontent that had spread among Middle Americans who felt left out of decisions and fed up with economic, cultural, and political changes taking place.

Less visibly, a democratic and progressive strand of citizen activism had also begun to develop among the same middle class constituencies of blue and white collar workers, small businesspeople, family farmers, and ethnics. Tens of thousands of community organizations and neighborhood associations sprang up across America. Activist groups multiplied among the elderly. Tens of thousands of citizens protested against escalating utility bills. A nuclear freeze movement emerged from crustily conservative New England town meetings. Caravans from every corner of the nation converged on Washington in the fall of 1985, bringing over a million signatures to demand cleanup of toxic waste. Farm organizations battling for the family farm sprouted across the South and Midwest like an early wheat crop.

In sum, two distinct and clashing strands of grass roots activism, one right wing, the other progressive, appealed to much the same base. Both argued that ordinary citizens had been left out of decisions. Both talked about jobs and workplaces, communities and neighborhoods, family, churches and synagogues, the American voluntary tradition. Both were often called—and sometimes described themselves as—populist. "The sometimes bewildering array of politicians who call themselves 'populist,'" wrote the *Congressional Quarterly*, "share the perception that there is tremendous political potential in an appeal to voters who feel trampled on and ignored by big institutions—corporations, government, unions, banks—and their representatives." [2]

Social movements often have contending wings. The American Revolutionary period produced both the Jeffersonian Democratic-Republicans and the Federalists. The Populists of the 1880s and 1890s led to a wave of cooperatives and black-white political alliances in the Deep South on the one hand and a long line of southern racist demagogues on the other. The social unrest of the Great Depression produced both the mass organizing campaigns that unionized American industry and the anti-Semitic diatribes of Father Coughlin. As in the past, two populist perspectives exist today as well.

Today, right wing populism uses the rhetoric of government as the enemy. It appeals to deep fears, a sense of despair, and a spirit of bitter competition between every group. Progressive populism offers a strikingly different alternative. It understands that for democracy to work we must have an educated, aroused, conscious, organized, and empowered citizenry. The populist vision is of an activist government that seeks to build self-reliance, promoting an extension of new democratic forms of participation, breaking down bureaucratic indifference. Citizens can use government to train, empower, organize, and teach, so that people are employed, day care centers are created, parents involved, communities organized, people encouraged and allowed to solve problems for themselves with the assistance of responsive public agencies. It fights to make government truly the "public servant" and big business accountable to communities where they are located and to the broader public interest. Progressive populism seeks to make democracy more than empty forms that can build powerlessness, frustration, and anger beneath the appearance of rule by the majority. The populist program is built around the effort to create a profound democratic reawakening that will give new direction to our communities, our economy, and government at all its levels.

Increasingly, the two branches of populism confront each other in the community, the legislature, the voting booth, and the halls of Congress. On the individual level neither right wing nor progressive populism often exists in a pure form. People may have one view on economic issues, another view on social issues, and another view on foreign policy. There is little that makes a person who supports toxic waste cleanup or lower utility rates necessarily favor affirmative action. People for nuclear disarmament don't necessarily support trade unions. But with all these complexities there are broad values and responses emerging that make two kinds of populism increasingly identifiable.

To those of us who are dismayed by the success of the New Right and believe its gains not to be in the best interest of the country, the possibilities often seem bewildering. On the one hand we are advised to become more like the right wing in order to gain the electoral support to oppose it. On the other hand we are told to stand firm and win people back to the old assumptions. Neither response is viable.

We are convinced that it is the new direction that emerges from grass roots progressive populism that can turn aside the offensive from the right wing and regain the initiative for the forces of democratic change. Progressive populism is nearing a position from which to challenge the dominance of the right not only on specific issues but also, more broadly, in terms of a basic vision for America's future. A brief sketch of the history of the right wing's success is useful for understanding both its vulnerabilities and the possibilities before us.

History: The Right's Rise to Power

The movement that elected Ronald Reagan didn't spring full blown from a television tube in 1979, nor was it the creation only of clever media specialists. Rather, its roots go back to 1964 and before.

When Senator Barry Goldwater lost the 1964 election to Lyndon Johnson, most observers thought his call for "extremism in defense of liberty" would appear afterward only in history books. But a group of young right wingers saw it differently. "Even if we did nothing but wear a Goldwater button or attend a rally—and some of the New Right are so young that is all they did," said Paul Weyrich, a key strategist of the movement, "that campaign left an indelible mark on us."

Many of Goldwater's issues were like those of other conservatives— lower taxes, less government regulation, a crusade against communism. But he also spoke to a feeling of growing discontent that would later be amplified by New Right populists. He claimed that "small men" at the top of society corrupted the principles they said they believed. He spoke about "the silent Americans who . . . cannot find voice against the mammoth organizations which mercilessly pressure their own membership." And he warned that cultural chaos was spreading. "There is violence in our streets, corruption in our highest offices, aimlessness among our youth, anxiety among our elders."[3]

Lyndon Johnson was able to gain support from those who feared Goldwater's readiness to use nuclear weapons as well as from supporters of the Civil Rights Movement. Many others opposed Goldwater's attacks on programs like Social Security. But despite Johnson's overwhelming victory, Goldwater had doubled his strength through the campaign. He had spoken to widespread feelings of being "silent" and "forgotten." And he identified "causes" in opposition to bureaucrats, communists, and protesters.

Right wingers adopted the message and learned new skills. "We learned how to stuff envelopes, ring doorbells, get out the vote on election day and contribute to a political campaign," wrote New Right fundraiser and organizer Richard Viguerie. "We also learned how to win a Presidential primary, how to select delegates to a national convention, how to put together a campaign team, how to use TV, radio and newspapers to communicate our message." Goldwater's campaign pioneered techniques for direct fundraising by mail. Richard Nixon, running for president in 1960, got contributions from 40,000 individuals. The number of contributors to Goldwater, many giving in small amounts, was over 660,000.

Most important, perhaps, the New Right learned a key fact of political power in America that has often eluded the experts: political clout is far less dependent upon the party system than upon broader social forces, groups, and movements that can mobilize people and have an impact on the system. The New Right began utilizing skills of electioneering. But, as Viguerie put it, it also discovered how to "go to the people at the grass roots for their help." There, it found a growing audience.[4]

Organizers like Viguerie developed direct mailing as a strikingly effective tool for fundraising and applying political pressure. In 1964, following the Goldwater campaign, Viguerie started his own company by copying 12,500 names from public records of Goldwater contributors. As his operations expanded, he came to see the many-sided nature of direct mail. "A letter may ask you to vote for a candidate," he wrote, "volunteer for campaign work, circulate a petition among your neighbors, write letters and postcards to your Senators and Congressmen." He saw the technique as "the advertising medium of the underdog," which allowed those outside the mainstream to get their message out.[5]

Direct mail techniques supported dozens of New Right single issue and political groups like the National Right to Work Committee, the National Rifle Association, the National Conservative Political Action Committee, and the American Security Council. And it proved a potent force in many fights.

The National Right to Work Committee, for instance, appealed to small business and others afraid of the power of Big Labor. In 1975 it targeted a piece of legislation, the common situs bill, that originally had broad bipartisan support. Under the bill, labor unions would have the right to picket construction sites that hired nonunion labor.

Right wingers reacted with vehemence. "Will you join me and 200,000 other Americans in launching this great crusade?" asked Congressman Mickey Edwards in a fundraising letter for the Conservative Caucus. He pledged to fight "to regain control of our government from the union boss-controlled radical politicians and bureaucrats."[6]

"Without direct mail," Viguerie later wrote, "President Ford would almost certainly have signed the common situs bill in January, 1976." But the National Right to Work Committee mailed out over four million letters asking for immediate protests to the White House. The appeal generated 720,000 letters and postcards, demanding a veto. Ford reversed himself on the legislation that he had promised his own secretary of labor. Unions were handed the first defeat on such a scale in decades. After Carter's election, this technique and other grass roots mobilization efforts were employed in fights around consumer protection, federal financing of elections, the SALT II Treaty, and proposed changes in the Hatch Act, which prohibits government employees from political participation.[7]

The right wing campaign against the Panama Canal Treaty in 1977 generated between seven and nine million pieces of direct mail and prepared the groundwork for a successful conservative challenge to liberal representatives in the 1978 elections. Like the fight around situs picketing, it also provided the occasion for flamboyant appeals and furthered the process of mobilizing grass roots networks like many fundamentalist churches. "I'm writing you as a personal messenger from God," declared the Reverend Billy James Hargis in a fund appeal. "He has shown me a way to set up a Christian line of defense in America." The National Conservative Political Action Committee asked, "What's next on the liberals' agenda? Do we give Alaska back to Russia and pay them at the same time?"[8]

It was not just that the right had brought the technology of direct mail to a new level. They had also developed a new message. During the Eisenhower years, the right had generally been the defenders of the American status quo ready to apply the brand of communist to anyone who questioned government policy. After Kennedy's election they changed from the most ardent supporters to the biggest critics, not just of specific government policy, but of the entire conception of activist government itself. It was here that they found massive popular support. Conversely, the liberals shifted from being outsiders to being government's principal defenders—a change that would prove their undoing.

History: The Liberals Lose Ground

With Lyndon Johnson's election in 1964, liberalism appeared triumphant. The economy was growing. More and more Americans believed that something should be done to include "the Other America" of the poor and disadvantaged groups in the expanding pie. And the

Civil Rights Movement claimed moral leadership of the nation with its call to "realize the promise of democracy."

Partly from expediency, partly from conviction, the Johnson administration responded to public sentiments. The president's proclamation that "we shall overcome" symbolized a new agenda for vitally important changes that included desegregation in public accommodations, protection of voting rights, consumer advocacy, poverty programs, housing efforts, expanded educational support, and many other initiatives. The social change program of the Great Society was often mired in administrative red tape and appeared bureaucratic in design. Moreover, its funding levels were often miserly and further eroded by an escalating war in Vietnam. And programs like the War on Poverty, originally conceived with a highly participatory flavor of "maximum feasible participation" by the poor, lacked the independently organized citizen base that could hold them accountable. But for all its weaknesses, the Great Society also illustrated much of the best of liberal politics. Its goals were not the problem, even though its methods fell short.[9]

Among the major weaknesses, the programs of the Great Society and much of mainstream liberalism generally became dangerously out of touch with the mood of Middle America. That mood included growing anger at economic, cultural, and political changes taking place, for which middle class Americans often had to foot the bill.

In the late 1940s, 70 percent of all American families could look forward to owning their own homes. In the 1960s, inflation began ravaging such dreams—by the end of the decade, only 30 percent of the population could afford new homes of their own. Values and institutions like church and synagogue, family, neighborhood, and country had given meaning and stability to lives of sacrifice and hard work. But they were called into question and even ridiculed by suddenly fashionable pundits who declared that "God is dead" and "all values are relative." Demonstrators burned the flag. Some denounced everyone "over 30."[10]

In this environment, growing numbers of citizens blamed "liberal elitists." In fact, liberalism is a rich, complex tradition, with democratic as well as technocratic elitist strands. But some elements within the liberal tradition did indeed warrant public skepticism. Since the 1930s, many of those who built the welfare state had been guided by the philosophy that the point of government was to act "on behalf of" the people. "The writer has faith," said Thurman Arnold, chief of the government's anti-trust division in the 1930s, "that the fanatical alignments between opposing political principles may disappear and a competent, practical and opportunistic governing class may rise to power." In the 1950s, liberal social scientists like Bernard Berelson celebrated the relative noninvolvement of most people in public life as a source of order and stability. By the Johnson administration, the idea of a "competent governing class" had firmly taken hold. In programs from health care to energy and education, ordinary citizens were supposed to be recipients, not participants. When Johnson declared before Congress that "we shall overcome," his foreign policy advisors were planning for a major escalation of the war in Vietnam—and discussing how to conceal such plans from the public.[11]

Social changes in the sixties added to the burdens of liberalism. In the context of a growing economic pie, Middle American whites could look with sympathy on the struggles and demands of the black underclass. But taxes for the Great Society fell most heavily on middle income taxpayers. By the end of the decade, the pie had stopped growing, and economic worries merged with white opposition to federal initiatives like busing.

Liberals, sensitive to the plight of the poor and minorities, at times gave the impression of insensitivity to the contributions of Lithuanians, Italians, Poles, Irish, and others. "What the hell does 'white' mean?" asked one ethnic man who protested the government's lumping of all those "of European descent" in its statistics. "They made *us* dig the tunnels," explained an Italian in Brooklyn. "When the earth caved in, it was always one of the Italians who died. Nobody of consequence! We were slaves."

Conservative strategists adroitly exploited such sentiments. According to author Kevin Phillips, "The Democratic Party fell victim to the ideological impetus of a liberalism which had carried it beyond programs taxing the few to the benefit of the many (the New Deal) to programs taxing the many on behalf of the few (the Great Society)." He argued that "the great political upheaval of the 1960s" would be "the populist revolt of the American masses . . . against the caste policies and taxation of the mandarins of Establishment liberalism."[12]

In 1968 George Wallace acted on this analysis. Wallace, the governor of Alabama, had gained publicity and become a hero to many southern whites by attempting to block the admission of blacks into the University of Alabama in 1963. After Wallace ran strongly in the 1964 Democratic primaries in northern states like Wisconsin, Indiana, and Maryland, his organizers geared up for an effort in 1968. They formed their own party, called the American Independent Party.

While extremist groups like the Ku Klux Klan, the John Birch Society, and the Minutemen played prominent roles at the local campaign level, Wallace posed as a populist who had supported labor unions and public works in Alabama. His audience, he argued, was "the average man in the street, this man in the textile mill, this man in the steel mill, this barber, the beautician, the policeman on the beat." And his main message was rage: at elite intellectuals, arrogant officials, ungrateful students, those who failed to support the boys in Vietnam. Wallace railed against "over-educated, ivory-tower folks with pointed heads looking down their noses at us." If elected, he promised to call in the bureaucrats and "take away their briefcases and throw them in the Potomac River." By late September, Wallace's strength was an astounding 38 percent in the polls in the South, compared with 31 percent for Nixon and 24 percent for Hubert Humphrey. Nationwide, his support stood at 21 percent, threatening to throw the election in a turmoil. Wallace's campaign sent a message: massive shifts in sentiment were occurring among blue and white collar Americans. Right wing organizers took heed. In many ways, political races were simply the tip of the iceberg for the emerging New Right movement.[13]

Another aspect in the decline of traditional liberalism was the entrance onto the political stage of a new generation for whom FDR and the New Deal was old history. The baby boom generation, those kids born in abnormally large numbers after World War II, grew up in the period of liberal political dominance. Vietnam turned them against cold war foreign policy associated with Lyndon Johnson as much as Richard Nixon. They distrusted big government and big bureaucracies of any kind. For most of this generation, the middle and late 1970s were a period of unique economic disappointments. To maintain a decent standard of living, an increasing number of younger families had to have two parents working. While they could in this manner keep their heads above the rising tide of inflation-driven bills, they often paid a heavy cost as parents and in the quality of their lives. For the first time, there was a growing sense that this new generation would not do better than their parents had. This fueled a longing for an exciting sense of new opportunity and direction. They turned toward a new face, a candidate who promised an outsider's approach rather than politics as usual.

Jimmy Carter's campaign for the presidency raised populist themes from a progressive point of view. Once in office, the new president responded to issues that grew out of neighborhood, consumer, and other progressive grass roots groups. For instance, Carter championed initiatives like the Home Mortgage Disclosure Act, through which neighborhoods could find out the pattern of bank lending in their areas. He backed the Consumer Protection Agency, long a chief objective of consumer activists. He appointed Monsignor Geno Baroni, Sam Brown, Marge Tabankin, Michael Pertshuk, Eleanor Holmes Norton, and many other citizen advocates to the administration.

But the Carter administration also reflected the liberal notion of government acting for the people, not involving them in decision making. The tax rate on corporations fell dramatically, while the middle income tax burden increased. Carter's Commission for a National Agenda for the Eighties calmly envisioned the abandonment of whole regions. It pronounced that supposedly "immutable . . . technological, economic, social and demographic trends" were leading to "a post-industrial society in which Boston, Cleveland and Detroit stand as 'bricks and mortar' snapshots of a bygone era." Alan Greenspan, former head of the Council of Economic Advisors under President Ford, saw "no significant difference" in the two administrations' economic approaches.[14]

But if it made "no difference" to observers at the pinnacles of economic power who held the nation's highest office, it made a great deal of difference down below. For the small business owner who found she paid more taxes than giant oil companies and whose interest rates paid to giant banks threatened her fragile independence, the debate was far from academic. For the laid off steel worker who discovered that his steel company had used its profits to acquire a circus instead of investing in renovations, the issue seemed less "immutable trends" than raw greed.

"We used to have biscuits and doughnuts and eggs and sausages and a big pot of coffee on Sunday morning," explained one housewife in Boston. "We just can't afford it any more. What we hoped for has turned into something else. It's like the beauty has been taken out of life. It's like it's all on the wrong speed."[15]

Liberalism, once America's guiding moral philosophy, became associated with a "do-your-own-thing" attitude that was seen as undermining the moral foundations of the society. "The focus on self has gone too far," Hazel Haralson Redding told *New York Times* reporter John Herbers at his thirty-fifth high school class reunion in Brownsville, Tennessee. "Love thyself, understand thyself, be sure of your own happiness and 'how to be No. 1'—all that is leading toward a self-centered society that loses all compassion and understanding of others." In a similar way, government and politics generally were seen as increasingly distant from the values and reach of ordinary citizens. "There's no accountability," despaired one woman in Ottumwa, Iowa. "There's no way to touch them. What can we do?" Even those aware of the critical importance of many government programs argued that government had too often slighted citizen initiative and independence. Carl Holman of the National Urban Coalition argued that black Americans "can't afford to lie back and wait for government. Much of our help has to come from our own community —churches, clubs, fraternities, sororities, fraternal orders and professional organizations."[16]

In sum, a decade or more of massive, sometimes violent changes had left the nation adrift and looking for different approaches. But the mood was far from that of a simple conservatism. Both Gallup and Harris polls found declining prejudice against blacks, women, and groups like gays and lesbians by the late 1970s. People favored more emphasis on values of family and religion—but also overwhelmingly believed that there should be "less emphasis on money."[17]

Public skepticism toward big business had grown stronger, even in conservative areas of the country. "It seems like when they get up there they think of the big man and forget about the little man," explained Mildred Baily, a beautician in the little town of Selma, North Carolina. By more than two to one, the public in 1975 believed that "America's major corporations tend to dominate and determine the actions of our public officials in Washington." Finally, there were widespread signs of a rebirth of American voluntary traditions. More and more Americans worked "off hours" in their communities, and the potential seemed barely tapped. Gallup polls discovered that 64 percent of the public was willing to "serve without pay" on voluntary committees that would address problems in their neighborhoods like schools, housing, health care, jobs, crime, and youth activity. The question was who would organize the popular discontent.[18]

Right wing populists were initially most successful in channeling such sentiments. Their main base—largely white and middle income—was far more homogeneous than progressive populists, who sought to build broad coalitions across often bitter lines of racial and income divisions. Such coalitions, in fact, took years to construct. Moreover, the right wing message was far simpler: it is always easy to offer scapegoats for people's feelings of victimization than to develop positive and effective strategies for citizen empowerment. And, in a world of enormous concentrations of wealth and power, any strategy for empowerment is likely to be greeted with enormous skepticism by many millions of citizens who have all but given up hope for democratic change. Finally, the New Right moved into political action far more quickly than did progressive populists. And in the 1980 elections, it found an effective and eloquent national spokesman.

Ronald Reagan had long voiced right wing populist themes. He had called for "an end to giantism" and charged that "thousands of towns and neighborhoods have seen their peace disturbed by bureaucrats and social planners through busing, questionable education programs, and attacks on family unity." In the race for the 1980 Republican nomination, his approach proved its power. John Connally, former treasury secretary, ran as the unabashed champion of big business—and was obliterated in Republican primaries. In contrast, Ronald Reagan called for a "populist coalition" and proclaimed himself the "champion not of the country club set but of the small businessman and the blue collar worker." The *Washington Post* found that "in sharp contrast to other Republicans, Reagan does substantially better with rank-and-file Republicans who seem skeptical about big business." The sparks that had been lit twelve years before suddenly burst into flame. "The party switch is secondary," said C. J. Harty, a former Wallace Democrat in North Carolina who ardently supported Reagan. "What's important is the philosophy. Your white ethnic voters, your blue-collar voters are going for Reagan. It's showing up everywhere." [19]

Right Wing Populism Destroys the Values It Claims to Champion

Throughout his presidency, Ronald Reagan has sounded like a populist. Thoughtful conservatives have made the point well. "Reagan's message," observes George Will, "has been more complex than the 'rugged individualism' of simple-minded conservatism." Rather, the president revived older American ideals of local control and institutions close to home. He argued that "the renaissance of the American community, a rebirth of the neighborhood, is the heart and soul of rebuilding America." In his State of the Union message in 1985, Reagan argued that his administration had led to a return to "the values we hold dear." "Progress," he maintained "began not in Washington, D.C., but in the hearts of our families, communities, workplaces and voluntary groups which, together, are unleashing the invincible spirit of one great nation under God." The president described his tax reform proposals for 1985 as a "new populism" that would "return economic power to the people." [20]

Whatever the fundamental flaws of the administration—and they are many—the themes that Ronald Reagan has brought back into public discourse ring true to huge numbers of Americans. Future politicians will ignore them at their peril. The use of these themes by the right may be demagogic, but people strongly believe in them and will vote for candidates who are perceived as standing for them. Other right wing themes, compelling at first hearing, on closer examination turn out to involve a narrow and restrictive definition of whom "the people" include. But even on its own terms, there is great irony in the populist tone of much of the administration's rhetoric.

President Reagan has often invoked the vision of America as a "city on the hill," as articulated by John Winthrop, the great seventeenth-century Puritan minister. But Winthrop warned more than 350 years ago that when avarice and unbridled individual ambition overtake public affairs, authentic community is impossible: "If our hearts shall ever turn away so that we worship the gods of profit and pleasure and follow them," he told his contemporaries, "we shall surely perish from this good land." For most Americans, the economic and social forces of recent years testify to the truth of Winthrop's warnings. Below the surface of the administration's glowing rhetoric, dramatic changes threatened the very foundations of the middle class. Right wing populism began to destroy the very values it claimed to champion.[21]

The administration claims to be returning initiative to the local level and encouraging voluntary activity to replace government programs, yet in practice it has shown a striking hostility toward independent, grass roots citizen initiatives and voluntary work. "We couldn't even get our phone calls answered," recounted Gary Hattem, director of the Saint Nicholas Neighborhood Preservation and Housing Rehabilitation Corporation, a community organization in Brooklyn that had revitalized its business and commercial strip. "It was like we were Godzilla after Reagan took office. Everyone in the bureaucracy ran in the other direction." Administration officials sought to abolish every government program that communities and local areas had found of most use in self-help and local self-organization. President Reagan gave an award for outstanding voluntary initiative to Sister Fattah of Philadelphia, inspirational leader of a youth shelter called the House of Umoja. Umoja had rehabilitated houses, begun anti-crime programs, and started an economic development project called Boystown Businesses to train unemployed teenagers. It also had to battle many unresponsive social service agencies and government bureaucracies to do so. But even as Reagan met with Sister Fattah, administration officials sought to block all the programs that Umoja had been able to use to revitalize its community and fight against unresponsive power.[22]

The pattern spread through every phase of the administration in ways people felt intuitively. "There's a deep concern that something is fundamentally wrong," described Barbara Mikulski, summarizing conversations with people in her Maryland congressional district. "The cop on the beat has to risk his life taking on the dope pushers and trying to survive the paper pushers. He pays more income taxes than General Electric a few blocks down the street which made a profit of $6 billion, laid off 635 workers and says it cannot compete. The elderly put their money into the savings and loans. They aren't high rollers or junk bonders. Right now that means their savings are at risk in my state. These are things people can picture, people can see." [23]

Reagan officials sought to override communities' rights to find out what toxic wastes local companies were generating. They attempted to deny federal funds to any area passing rent control legislation. Their tax ideas put at risk every voluntary organization in America. "Every kind of organization from museums and colleges to small neighborhood associations or advocacy groups is aroused about the Administration's policies toward charities," observed Brian O'Connell, president of the Independent Sector, a coalition of 595 national nonprofit groups. Even the president's New Federalism, hall... rk of his call to "return power to the people," died as a result of administration neglect and intransigence, according to local and state political analyst Neal Peirce.[24]

A Politics of Powerlessness, Tinsel, and Greed

Right wing populism appeals to many who feel threatened by changes and unable to do much about them. Religious fundamentalists are outraged by the violence and degradation so widespread in the mass media. Small businesspeople feel their dreams of independence are being threatened by giant conglomerates. Young couples fear they will never get homes of their own. Baby boomers are told they must accept not doing as well as their parents. For young people whose college educations seemed only to be preparing them for working in clerical or fast food occupations the right offered a vision of an unshackled American economy where there would once again be no limits on growth or on dreams. For those worried about foreign economic competition and the decline in U.S. world stature, the right offered new patriotism. The base of right wing populism is varied. But the way it channels discontent has three identifiable features.

POWERLESSNESS. Populism itself always grows from people's sense of being powerless. The right wing has drawn a great deal of its success from its ability to name such an experience and portray conventional liberalism as the politics of the elite. But right wing populism is a politics of powerlessness. It speaks to people's experiences of being victimized by large institutions, but it suggests little serious strategy for regaining control over government or business. Rather, right wing populism proposes that "real leaders" be substituted for the false leaders of the people. It looks to others for rescue. By way of contrast, progressive populism aims at empowerment.

TINSEL ROOTS. Populism is a politics of "roots," of attachment to hometown values, religious commitments, traditions like American voluntarism. The New Right has also drawn considerable power from its rhetorical championing of such roots and from its charges that liberals had become uprooted cosmopolitans who had no interest in these values. But in right wing terms, such ideas become exclusionist, illusory, and rigid. Right wing populism assumes a narrow definition of "the people"—generally white, Anglo-Saxon Protestants. It makes scapegoats of others who fall outside, from single mothers to Latin immigrants, and blames them for "the people's" problems.

Appealing to the widespread feeling of loss of community, right wing populism proposes a return to an imagined past, when everybody "knew their place" and people were more neighborly, patriotic, and concerned about their families. It seeks to impose rigid moral absolutes on issues that range from what books kids should read in school to the proper place of women. Progressive populism defends and celebrates a healthy, diverse, and pluralist sense of "roots," those hometown values closest to us that are expressed in different ways by different communities.

GREED. Finally, populism always expresses a vision of the American Dream. Again, the New Right has often invoked the American Spirit in contrast to the supposed detachment of liberals from a deep identification with the country. But the right wing vision of America celebrates a dog-eat-dog morality that leads toward increasing division.

In the terms of the original Populists and subsequent popular leaders in their tradition, like Martin Luther King, Jr., the American Dream was a shared one. America was seen as a "commonwealth." Private property was never an end in itself. As Benjamin Franklin put it, property was simply "the creature of society," and those who held it had a deep obligation to act as stewards for the general good.

Right wing populism sometimes rails against big business. But its true message is illustrated best by its approach to America's economic, natural, and cultural riches. Simply, right wing populism has a selfish understanding of the American Dream. Thus it joins with Big Business in an assault to take over for private use all our forms of "commonwealth," from our natural resources and national parks and wilderness areas to the Federal Housing Administration, which Reagan recently announced that he would like to sell to a private buyer. (The FHA has shown a profit of about $7 billion a year recently.) The person of vast riches is the model of success, even the object of divine grace. As Jerry Falwell expressed such a view, "Riches are the Lord's way of blessing those who put Him first." In contrast, progressive populism seeks to rebuild a sense of our "common wealth." It challenges the selfishness of large corporations, which squander their capital on speculation, mergers, and foreign investments, when so much of our own industry needs modernization and our communities need to be revitalized by local investment. [25]

Toward a Progressive Vision
of Democracy and Political Power

The original Populist movement was a revolt by small farmers who sought to save farms, communities, and ways of life that were threatened by big banks and other large institutions. Populists had ideas of self-government like those of America's founding fathers and mothers. They distrusted concentrated power in corporations and government alike. And they saw in America's voluntary tradition the only enduring bulwark of liberty.

The heart of the first movement was hope, connected to practical and effective action. Populists believed that changes could actually be brought about in unresponsive government, that farms and rural communities could actually be saved from ruthless lenders and greedy local merchants. The Populists put their convictions into practice. They formed thousands of cooperatives, called the Alliances, through which they bought supplies and marketed their goods. Historian Alan Brinkley has described the first movement as "the constructive efforts of thousands of communities to build institutions and establish values that would permit an alternative economy (and alternative value system) . . . to the competitive, centralizing tendencies of industrial capitalism." When people act out of hope—and seek alliances with other groups of the powerless— they also are often able to demonstrate a spirit of generosity, tolerance, and inclusiveness. Thus, although not without prejudices, the first Populists were also remarkably daring on issues, speaking out to improve black-white relations and the role of women, far in advance of any other major southern movement in the nineteenth century. The Populist vision, in sum, was democratic empowerment, democratic roots, and a democratic view of the commonwealth.[26]

This vision resonates today with increasing numbers of Americans. It offers a perspective and some guiding principles with roots that go back a hundred years, yet are uniquely suited to the new period we have entered. The pace of change is accelerating at a staggering rate. Our economy and technology experience radical changes affecting how we live. We are going through a set of transformations as profound as the industrial revolution that fundamentally shaped the last three hundred years of history. But the current revolution is proceeding at a faster pace, compressing into a single decade mammoth alterations that in the past would have stretched over a century.

These developments hold out enormous possibilities for improvement in our lives. We can travel to the moon. We can produce more goods. We can even grow plants that resist their natural enemies. We can manipulate the very substances of life itself to produce new medicines.

But as wondrous as they are, technological innovations don't guarantee a future that we will be proud of. Wonder drugs cannot check the spreading cancers from the toxic wastes already poisoning our air, earth, and water. Wonder plants will not save the midwestern family farmer, nor necessarily get to the starving African family. More products from fewer workers may not mean more leisure but the hardship of unemployment.

Today it is vital to reaffirm basic principles that will allow us to extend and improve the democratic promise of America. We must be stewards of the land, of the wealth, and of our unique democratic system, preserving, caring for, and nurturing them for future generations. That is why restoring "commonwealth" understanding is so urgently needed.

Short-sighted greed, allowed to run rampant over the public interest, can damage even the best democracy. Now in a society in the turmoil of rapid change, we have the technologies to magnify the effects of narrow greed into cataclysmic disasters. Only by building a politics of public morality, based on our democratic roots, can we be the good stewards of our commonwealth.

Technology must be made to serve the needs of the vast majority. Inevitably the existing trends that merge our economy and people into a more global society will accelerate. But this internationalization need not be at the expense of whole regions and constituencies. Nor should it or need it threaten the unique characteristics that have made America so special. But the positive future that is possible is not inevitable.

The key to our future lies in new forms of social organization. Only if we can unleash our human power can we ensure that technology and rapid change make our future brighter. Democratic empowerment, a rediscovery of our democratic roots, and a democratic view of the commonwealth remain vibrant lights by which we can guide our nation's voyage into a tumultuous future.

By contrast right wing populism is the image without the reality, the stuff of illusions and magic. Despite its professions of hope for America's future, in fact it is born of deep despair about the possibilities of serious, substantive democracy. But ordinary people can overcome even the most devastating feelings of powerlessness through experiences in which they learn new skills and are able to act with effectiveness, dignity, and independence.[27]

2. PROGRESSIVE POPULISM
The Politics of Empowerment

*Ours is a nation in crisis. America, born of hope, now is becoming
a society overwhelmed by fear. But we refuse to submit to selfishness
or the fashionable cynicism that nothing can be done. We refuse to tell
our children and grandchildren that the only time worth living was
before they were born. The past will not come again. We need
change. We need a profound democratic awakening.*

Citizen Action, 1982 Program

I n the 1970s and 1980s, the same economic and social developments
that gave rise to right wing populism also began to shape a progressive populist movement. In the process of organized struggle on a wide
range of issues from tenant rights to plant closing legislation and from
neighborhood development to blocking utility rate increases, tens of
thousands of citizens have begun to find a voice and gain a sense of
power. On the foundation of their activity, an organizational and electoral alternative to the right has now begun to emerge.

In the mid-1980s, America is a world away from the rural commu-
nities of the nineteenth century. But once again, one hundred years after
the first Populist revolt, a progressive populist perspective is emerging in
American life and politics. Public figures like Senators Tom Harkin,
Albert Gore, and Paul Simon; congressional leaders like Lane Evans,
Barbara Mikulski, Marcy Kaptur, and Jim Weaver; black leaders like

the Reverend Jesse Jackson, Charles Hayes, Maxine Waters, and Al Wheat of Kansas City; state and local officials like Henry Cisneros, mayor of San Antonio, Jim Hightower, Texas secretary of agriculture, and Raymond Flynn, mayor of Boston—all are described as populist or use the term in self-description.

Progressive populism mounts serious challenge to elites. And it aims at popular control over corporate and bureaucratic institutions that have gotten out of control. As Senator Harkin, co-chair of the new Congressional Populist Caucus, summarizes: "Freedom and democratic institutions rest on the widest possible dissemination of wealth and power— and we've come to the point where too few people have too much and the rest of us have too little." [1]

Moreover, like the first Populists, populist politics today is in many ways simply the tip of the iceberg, the reflection of a much broader and deeper social force. Progressive populism's foundations are to be found in a rebirth of citizen action efforts that have spread at the grass roots in recent years. Community organizations like Communities Organized for Public Service in San Antonio have transformed local politics, giving poor and powerless people a major voice in decision making for the first time. COPS and other similar groups affiliated with the network called the Industrial Areas Foundation have served as models for large scale local populist coalitions like San Francisco Organizing Project and many others. Networks like the Federation of Southern Cooperatives, Center for Third World Organizing, and Mississippi Action for Community Education (MACE) have proved an enduring, vital legacy of the Civil Rights Movement. National alliances like Citizens for Tax Justice, National People's Action, the National Congress of Neighborhood Women, and Association of Community Organizations for Reform Now (ACORN) have brought together for the first time blacks, Hispanics, and white ethnics in hundreds of areas around issues of common concern. Working women's groups, public interest and consumer networks, peace groups, and grass roots environmental campaigns that range from Clean Water Action Project to Citizens for a Better Environment and Greenpeace are also part of the new citizen force taking shape.

The chapters that follow are about the political, social, and economic alternative that begins to emerge from grass roots citizen activism. They are told especially from the point of view of Citizen Action, one of the leading organizations in the new progressive populism. Citizen Action's roots lie in state-wide organizations created in the early 1970s. At that time, many community organizers realized that, in part because of the fiscal crises of the cities, the solutions to many community problems often required action at the state and national level. This was especially true for larger problems such as energy costs, environmental hazards, economic instability, and jobs. After a period of triumphant conservatism, few had predicted the rise of progressive citizen opposition. But few had earlier predicted the rise of right wing populism. During the seventies, progressive populist organizations, grounded in local areas and coordinating campaigns on state and national levels, expanded rapidly.

The Citizen Action method of organizing has power because, like progressive populism generally, it takes up issues having the potential for uniting many different types of people and gaining majority support. It combines grass roots organizing in communities with electoral tactics. It builds permanent staffed organizations and coalitions that often include senior citizens, unions, neighborhood, tenant, and ethnic organizations, churches, women's groups, environmentalists, and consumers. It does not hesitate to go outside of the established channels in its efforts to challenge unresponsive corporations and public bureaucracies. Citizen Action, however, does not mount fights out of automatic hostility to government, the hallmark of the New Right. Rather, like the progressive populist movement of which it is a part, it revives the oldest American dream of self-government. It takes seriously the notion of "government of the people, by the people, and for the people," insisting on the necessity of each element.

"I explain the Indiana Citizen Action Coalition as an organization of ordinary people," said Chuck Deppert, a leader of the group and co-chair of national Citizen Action. "It gives people a voice in matters they otherwise wouldn't have had a voice about. That's what we stand for."[2]

Let us introduce some of these "ordinary people."

Philip Frazeur, a retired metalworker in Griswold, Iowa, had always believed in working hard, meeting one's obligations, and making a contribution. In 1981, he had been married forty-three years. His youngest child was in college. But he was worried. Frazeur's modest income was fixed; his gas bills had jumped in recent years—from forty-eight dollars for a hundred cubic feet of gas in 1975 to sixty-two dollars in 1980. Spending several hundred dollars to insulate his house, he also put in dozens of hours of his own work fixing the attic roof, foundations, doors, and windows. His gas consumption dropped by 50 percent. "I thought this would be a sure way to get a smaller fuel bill," he remembered. But bills continued to skyrocket, rising to $104. By the end of 1983, Frazeur and his wife feared they would soon face a choice "between utilities and food" during cold Iowa winters.

The story was much the same across the country, in the wake of loosening of federal controls on energy prices. Between 1978 and 1983, typical residential price increases were 122 percent in Detroit, 102 percent in Washington, and 257 percent in Los Angeles. For thousands of Americans, as basic a necessity as heating threatened to become an out-of-reach luxury item. In 1983, utilities cut off three hundred thousand families because they could not pay their bills. Oil companies pressed confidently ahead with plans to decontrol gas prices completely. The Reagan administration pledged its full support. But people like Philip Frazeur, in response, mounted the largest sustained consumer revolt in the nation's history. Organized by the Citizen Labor Energy Coalition, allied with Citizen Action, the effort to keep controls on natural gas prices contacted over fifteen million American homes. It collected more than three million signatures. Through intensive lobbying, demonstrations, scores of "accountability sessions," and meetings between large groups of voters and members of Congress, the Energy Coalition blocked complete decontrol of natural gas prices in 1980.[3]

When the auctioneer arrived at the Randall Carson farm in central Illinois to sell off family possessions to cover debts, a crowd of two hundred men dressed in blue jeans and windbreakers shouted him down. "No sale! No sale!" they chanted, using portable loudspeakers. Worried about what would happen next, the local sheriff cancelled the sale. On the surface, it seemed simply another in a series of rural actions that swept across the Midwest and South in the middle years of the 1980s, as farmers desperate to retain their lands banded together to fight against banks and merchants, like the Populists of old. But this crowd had a difference. Through the efforts of groups like the Illinois Farm Alliance, an affiliate of the state-wide Illinois Public Action Council and Citizen Action, it represented a new sort of coalition. In the front rows were members of the United Automobile Workers union, many of whom had driven for hours to attend in a show of solidarity with farmers. "We will never forget them," said Susan Carson. "We thought we were alone." It was not an isolated incident. "From Ohio to Colorado and up to the Dakotas," reported the *New York Times*, "urban unions and rural farmers are daily forging new organizational links and personal bonds. This burgeoning movement, a contemporary echo of the emotional and potent Populist past, is starting to construct its own economic agenda and a strong sense of shared identity among union members and farmers who see their life as a struggle against powerful big interests."[4]

Cora Tucker, Citizen Action co-chair and daughter of a sharecropper in Halifax, Virginia, had long been sustained by her faith in the Lord and the support of the black community as she battled racial segregation through the sixties and seventies. But in the 1980s, she faced problems of housing, education, jobs, and pollution bigger than blacks alone could handle. Small farmers were losing their land. Mining companies were planning to dig throughout the state for open pit excavations of uranium. Scientists warned that groundwater tables might well be contaminated and crops and animal life poisoned. Worried about the growing threat, Tucker joined with an interracial alliance called Southside Concerned Citizens that blocked the uranium companies from opening the mines. Tucker went on to help organize an interracial state-wide group, Virginia Action, that worked on issues ranging from voter registration to utility rates.[5]

The new progressive populism of the 1980s grew from the actions of millions of citizens like Philip Frazeur, the United Automobile Workers members, and Cora Tucker, who have become convinced of the need for action to get the voice and the power to do something about problems of job loss, prices, threats to neighborhoods from toxic waste, and the loss of family farms. Often citizens have joined with others with whom they previously thought they had little in common. "The unions, whose membership is dwindling, and the family farmers, whose numbers are dwindling, don't need to fight over the table scraps," explained Charles Williams, a Machinists union leader. "If we don't work together, in fifteen years you'll have a few food conglomerates controlling all our supplies, like the oil companies." What began simply as questions of self-interest, moreover, often developed into more lasting bonds. Dick Steffen, a farmer outside Waterloo, Iowa, explained that he had never known city residents well before. "But they're all right. Every chance I get I tell my friends how these guys are entitled to a decent wage just like us. Little by little, people get educated. The barriers are crumbling."[6]

The problems of forging a common progressive populist movement, however, are formidable. Citizens today suffer from enormous discouragement that anything can be done to affect large institutions of government and business. Equally, the difficulties of building a common movement are immense in a nation that reflects the diversity of the whole world.

Americans, unlike their counterparts in other nations, do not share a single "tradition." Each of the myriad peoples who have come to our shores (or who have been forcibly brought) has a particular story, a unique experience, and a distinctive outlook. American history has been often the history of bitter conflict among different groups. In periods of growing economic instability, the pressures toward division quickly worsen. Often those in power play one group off against the next.

Yet the diverse people of America do share certain basic aspirations and values, across all the differences. They hold strongly to commitments to family, however defined by different groups. They believe in hard work, determination, independent livelihood. Most share a faith in God —and hold dear the values of Judeo Christian tradition including the sacredness of the individual, stewardship of the earth, and justice for all people. Aside from the most mobile and rootless, Americans hold strongly to values of community and locality, to one's native or adopted hometown. Finally, most people see themselves as members of larger groups, whether racial, religious, ethnic, or, for some, occupational. Such groups are formed by common interests and values. They often are defined by a common heritage of struggle for dignity, voice, and recognition by the broader society.

As people organize and take on larger issues, they frequently find that they simply don't have the power in their own communities, organizations, or workplaces to win. They are forced to ally with others. They attend meetings with people with whom they never thought they would associate. They work on committees and visit the homes and neighborhoods of others very different from themselves. In the course of organizing, they often learn that what brings them together is stronger than what keeps them apart.

Obviously, there are some points of deep division in our society that will not be bridged in the foreseeable future, particularly where religious beliefs put people on different sides of a question, abortion and gay rights for example. Some people can agree to disagree, but others can not. Often these are manipulated and exploited by politicians and preachers. It is here where groups like People for the American Way are important to defend a pluralist and open conception of American life.

At the moments of great democratic movement in American history, people from different heritages and groups have been able to find common ground on the basis of shared values and shared interests. Today, discovery of such common ground has proved to be the challenge of the emerging progressive populist movement.

That challenge is more urgent than at any other time in recent history. We face a future in which all the trends point to greater fragmentation of our society. Increasingly, the problems of a black youth in Newark can be isolated from the problems of a young two-wage-earner family in Cleveland Heights, which can be isolated from the problems of a family farmer in Bismark, which in turn can be isolated from the problems of the high tech engineer concerned with toxic wastes in the Silicon Valley. Not only do the problems seem isolated, but we no longer seem to have a sense of public morality and common purpose. The internationalization of our economy, the deep social and economic transformation engendered by rapid technological change, the accelerated growth of mammoth corporate structures, all can tend to further fragment our nation. Progressive populism offers a vision of the commonwealth, common ground that can unite a fractured society not through demagogic appeals or nostalgia, but for a common good rooted in the deepest values of our culture applied to a changing and uncertain future.

It would be wrong to romanticize the point: in a society so deeply divided along lines of race, culture, gender, age, and class, achievement of a genuine spirit of "one from many" is often very difficult to achieve. Sometimes, it can occur only around temporary issue alliances. At other times, the best that can be hoped for is to defuse an explosive antagonism. For example, some racial divisions may not easily be resolved, but new trust between people can be created by working across color lines on a common problem.

Progressive populism at its best looks beyond marriages of convenience to an older American vision. It seeks to realize the Dream of Martin Luther King, Jr., for an America where "blacks and whites, Jews and Gentiles, Protestants and Catholics can join hands" in a common commitment to freedom. Such a cultural, political, and economic vision affirms our shared values and community institutions like church and synagogue, family, voluntary group, or labor union local as central to a full life and an active democracy. It also appreciates the diverse forms such institutions take and the ways in which, necessarily, they evolve and change.

Unlike the right wing, which preaches a dog-eat-dog form of competition and a radical privatism, populism revives the central view of economics articulated by our nation's founders like Benjamin Franklin, Mercy Warren, and Thomas Jefferson. It holds that all forms of economic enterprise and private property, from businesses to family farms, are charges over which we are stewards for the broader community. And it argues for a "public interest" that can sustain our shared forms of wealth, from park lands to public libraries. It maintains a common responsibility for the poor, the oppressed, and the excluded, seeing the nation's commitments to principles of "liberty and justice for all" as a crucial measure of our "commonwealth."[7]

These are themes that combine self-interest with an idealism that calls on us to be more than we are. They wed the "hometown values" closest to us with a broader vision. There is nothing easy or simple about reviving such principles in a world that, in many ways, is organized on profoundly different principles. "Might Makes Right" and "Look Out for Number One" are the slogans and headlines on paperback books and in the daily news. But the principles of a progressive populism are, nonetheless, core themes that have surfaced again and again in our history.

Social movements are special events in history. They occur when problems that have long been beneath the surface suddenly boil up and sweep large numbers of people into action. In the years just before social movements start, there are usually profound economic and demographic changes. The old Populism grew out of the transition to modern urbanized America and an economy dominated by large corporations. It was an effort, especially by small farmers, to preserve their communities and their farming way of life.

Today's right wing populism and progressive populism both emerge from deep social and economic transformations as well. These changes raise basic questions of who suffers, who benefits, who controls, and whose values shape our future. The shifts from a manufacturing economy to a service economy, from a national economy to a global economy, and from localized corporations to dominant multinationals threaten the livelihood and well-being of millions of people. In the process, these changes threaten to destroy many forms of community, fairness, security, and dignity that people have created and sustained in the twentieth century.

In the 1970s, wrenching economic changes began to trouble the dreams of Middle Americans. Below the surface, transformations in the economy reshaped the terms of the economic debate.

World War II had greatly strengthened America's economic position in the world. The result was twenty years of relative prosperity, during which the living standard of the average American rose steadily. Not only did many individuals expect to make more money each year, but also each generation expected to do better than had its parents.

In 1968 the postwar economic expansion ended. The American standard of living stopped its annual rise and became stagnant. The causes were twofold. First, the economy of Europe had been restored, and Japan and Germany emerged as major industrial competitors. Second, during the years when there was little competition to worry about, American business became shortsighted. Investment in new plants was neglected so that industries such as steel and automobiles entered the 1970s with the same equipment they had been using in the 1930s. Investment in research and development was also neglected. The large profits flowing from military contracts focused the best American talent in that direction. Corporations failed to keep up in applying new technology to consumer markets the way competitors did.

Big business had an answer, developed in new organizations like the Business Roundtable, which brought chief executives together to plan strategy and take action. Their strategy had five parts: (1) force wage concessions from working people and weaken the power of unions generally; (2) end government regulation, particularly in the areas of environmental protection, health, safety, and race and sex discrimination; (3) lower taxes on corporations and taxes on the rich, while shifting the burden still further onto the middle class; (4) reduce the then-rampant inflation by cutting federal spending; (5) move as much high wage American production as possible to low wage parts of the world. In an outspoken editorial in 1974, *Business Week* summed it up:

> It will be a hard pill for many Americans to swallow—the idea of doing with less so that big business can have more. It will be particularly hard to swallow because it is quite obvious that if big business and big banks are the most visible victims of what ails the Debt Economy, they are also in large measure responsible for it.[8]

Business Week's point that big business bore an important measure of responsibility for the problems was well taken. American corporations claimed that they lacked the capital to modernize, but the facts were different. The amount of money available for investment was greater than at any other time in the years since World War II, but as economists Robert Reich and Ira Magaziner observed, "It is the way [resources] are committed that is crucial." In the case of steel, for instance, a large investment led to relatively little gain in productivity because it had gone mainly toward marginal plants, aimed at obtaining quick increases in capacity, rather than in long term programs for modernization. Losing ground to steel industries in Japan and Europe, the American companies began a series of massive layoffs that were to devastate the steel producing communities of the nation.

There existed other possibilities. In much of Western Europe, for example, workers and communities had a variety of inputs into business decision making. In West Germany, Austria, the Netherlands, and other nations, worker representatives by law held as many as half the seats on corporate boards, with full rights to debate and vote on corporate policies. If businesses were seen as responsible to the communities in which they were located, decisions about plant shutdowns, environmental pollution, or reinvestment could not be made apart from their actual impact on human beings.

But the politics of the workplace and the economy in America rested upon another approach. One might give one's life to General Motors, but there was no thought of reciprocity from the company's side. Although citizens and communities often enough paid for research and development, roads, sewer lines, and a host of other services indispensable to business, it was assumed that obligations were not returned. The "commonwealth" was forgotten. Neither the public nor the community itself, according to the new economic theories, had a right to be involved. Businesses were described, favorably, as "revolutionaries and radicals" that swept away all old-fashioned obligations.[9]

As the economic problems of the 1970s grew, corporations missed the easy profits of the 1950s and 1960s. Under intense pressure from stockholders to maintain the "bottom line," corporate executives found that it was often easier to make profits through speculation than by producing a product. The problem was that the entire thrust of the corporate approach to America's economic problems discouraged longer term thinking. "We all know of people all over this town who are running their companies into the ground," said one executive recruiting officer in New York, "taking huge, quick profits and leaving them a shell."[10]

Speculation of every sort had rapidly increased. Lending patterns of the largest banks meant a piling of loan onto loan in foreign markets that created what banking economist Martin Mayer called "phantasmagorical banks," in which profits were merely reported but not in reality earned. By the end of the decade, the United States had more invested in mortgages than in all businesses added together. A merger boom began to gather speed rapidly. Instead of reinvesting in the steel industry, U.S. Steel acquired Marathon Oil.

Between 1980 and 1985, American corporations spent $380 billion on mergers and acquisitions. Patterns of concentration reflected such merger activity. By 1979, the Fortune 500—the five hundred largest manufacturing corporations, representing 0.02 percent of all American companies —accounted for more than 80 percent of all manufacturing sales and more than 75 percent of profits. The four top firms controlled 93 percent of sales in automobile production, 90 percent in electric lamp production, and 87 percent in copper production. The assets of the largest two hundred matched the percentage of the economy held by the largest one thousand in 1941.[11]

The Reagan administration has touted entrepreneurship and small business. Mainstreet businessmen and businesswomen calculated, rightly, that they were the source of most new jobs and innovation in the economy. Despite the rhetoric, administration policies dramatically favored the largest corporations. Nationally syndicated columnist Neal Peirce reported that, in the 1970s, the largest one thousand corporations exported overseas about as many new jobs as they created. In contrast, small businesses with fewer than twenty employees created two thirds of all new jobs. But 80 percent of the Reagan tax breaks for business went to the top 0.1 percent of American firms, the giants of the economy. As a result of Reagan's tax cuts and changes, large firms—with one billion dollars or more in sales—got 61 percent of their federal taxes covered by credits, while small firms—with one million to five million dollars in sales—had only 6.5 percent of their taxes covered.[12]

Ten years after it had argued that Americans had to do with less "so that big business can have more," *Business Week* editorialized that the growing focus among corporate executives on the short term threatened disaster: "Fewer start up operations, less development of new products . . . or oil fields and more service businesses at the expense of capital-intensive manufacturing could add up to the slow 'deindustrialization' of the U.S." "If the trend continues," said one managing partner of a leading investment bank, "it means economic suicide."[13]

There were immediate human costs. What had earlier happened to blacks, Hispanics, and then women began to happen to millions of white males as well. Reaganomics closed factories across the country,

often for good. In December, 1981, the fabled U.S. Steel plant in Brad-
dock, Pennsylvania—the Edgar Thompson Works, known as E.T.—
closed for good. "My father worked at E.T. for forty years," said Tom
Medved, a thirty-nine-year-old roller in the slab mill who himself had
worked there nineteen years and 364 days. "My uncles and cousins all
worked there. It was the natural thing to do." A job in the company was
supposed to be secure for life. But more than a year later, Medved still
had not found a regular job, and his family, including four children,
struggled to make it on supplementary unemployment benefits. Meanwhile, in Rockford, Illinois, George Papson, a fifty-year-old machinist
who had come to the states from Greece as a young child after his father
had been killed by the Nazis, was laid off from his job with ten minutes'
notice. "I wanted to live in heaven on earth; that is why I came to
America," he explained. "I came here. I worked thirty years. I became
middle class. I can take a piece of metal in my hands and make it match
a blueprint within a tolerance of half a thousandth of an inch. Now I
can't find a job. What will happen to me?"

The question "What will happen to me?" began echoing through Middle America. "All over America's industrial heartland," reported *Newsweek* in 1983, "the national faith in prosperity forever is fading. In its
place are the brute realities of silent machinery and boarded-up store-
fronts, of once proud men and women waiting in welfare lines." The
administration promised a "recovery" that did, indeed, affect large areas
of the country. But longer range changes at work made no area safe and
secure in the long run.[14]

Conglomerates by their nature consist of collections of many separate
and unrelated companies, "bought and sold like so many trinkets in a
bazaar," as two economists observed. Local firms are gobbled up by
corporate manipulators who may never have even seen them. Factory
towns in New England, the Midwest, even "boom town" areas of the
Sunbelt states, found themselves at the mercy of distant decisions makers.
Many were abandoned, like the "hometown" described by Bruce Springsteen:

Now Main Street's whitewashed windows and vacant stores
seems like there ain't nobody wants to come down here no more

They're closing down the textile mill across the railroad tracks
Foreman says these jobs are going boys
   and they ain't coming back to your hometown [15]

Company managers were transferred from place to place too quickly to sink roots or become involved in local community affairs. Their children's schools were not dependent upon the company for their tax base. Their local church did not live in the shadow of a smokestack that would cease breathing its industrial life if investment opportunities turned out to be "more promising in Singapore." Fewer and fewer top executives had actual experience in the product lines or services the companies engaged in. Branches became simply "profit centers," for producing capital that could be invested in profitable, quick return ventures. In sum, the measure of an economy dominated increasingly by giant corporations is its increasing detachment from actual people and the communities in which they live.

By the mid-eighties, *Newsweek* had dubbed the decade "the age of cowboy capitalism"; *Business Week* termed America a "casino society." Many corporate executives themselves had begun to organize against the "merger mania" that threatened America's economic foundations.

For ordinary Americans, consequences were specific, concrete, and often destructive of life long dreams and aspirations. A family in Detroit or Pittsburgh that previously "made it" on one income saw both partners working. For single parents, the number of hours they had to work to feed the children increased from forty to fifty or fifty-five or sixty. In the 1970s, increases in employment in food service—restaurants and bars, primarily—had been greater than the total employment in the automobile and steel industries combined. Nationwide, 70 percent of the jobs were in service, which paid about 83 percent of the wages of manufacturing.[16] The United States increasingly was moving toward a two-tier society, in which an expanding layer of workers were trapped in low paid, less skilled, and dead end jobs. The backbone of America's middle class jobs—industries like steel, automobiles, machine tools, construction, and mining—were eroding. From 1979 to 1983, more than four million jobs in manufacturing were lost permanently. In the fall of 1985, the Joint Economic Committee of Congress released a study that found middle class incomes, in real terms, had fallen more than 11 percent over the preceding decade—with almost all the decline occurring since 1979. Meanwhile, the top 10 percent of American families received 29 percent of all personal income in 1969, 32 percent in 1976, and 33 percent in 1982.[17]

These figures are not inevitable consequences of "the free market" or "progress." Rather, they grow from specific decisions made by those who advance their own narrow special interests. As these economic trends and corporate policies unfolded, citizens began to organize for a defensive battle. Incomes were under attack, but taxes kept rising. Unemployment refused to go down, good jobs were lost and replaced by low paying jobs. As plants were closing and jobs moving away from many parts of the country, federal aid and revenue sharing funds were cut back. Communities suffered, schools suffered, health care suffered, and good housing became unaffordable. The middle class struggled to hold its own. Some people moved toward right wing populism and others toward progressive populism at times depending on nothing more than who got to them first.

At the same time that the lives of traditional blue collar industrial workers grew increasingly more uncertain, a new generation of Americans came of age. The women and men of the baby boom who started to reach their peak earning years in the late seventies and early eighties were in many respects quite different from their parents. They had no memories of the Great Depression, of Roosevelt, of neighbors being saved from eviction by radical groups, or of the organizing drives of the CIO. They did not share the experience of being lifted from poverty to the middle class by trade unionism. Many of them grew up in the suburbs rather than in close ethnic urban communities. The church was much less the social center of their lives; the lodge and the social club that celebrated the language of their grandparents were left behind. Their families were scattered across the country wherever the search for jobs took them. They owed no particular loyalty to either political party and the conventional labels of liberal and conservative rarely applied to them in a meaningful way. (Indeed, those who had been influenced by the social movements of the 1960s remember the then incumbent Democrats, not the Republicans, as the problem.) Referred to as the "New Collar" class, they work primarily in the service industries. They are on the whole better educated than their parents, but will not enjoy as high a standard of living as an industrial job in a unionized plant brought to the older generation.

On many issues the baby boom "New Collar" generation may be at odds with its elders. For example, they see higher industrial wages as the cause of higher prices that they must pay. They don't benefit from trade protection, but enjoy buying low priced, high quality foreign imports. Unlike those industrial workers who believe that "no smoke means no work," they have more to gain from environmental protection. Many of them get no employment boost from high military spending. Seeing how often government doesn't work for them, a government program is not the first thing that comes to their minds to solve a social problem. They may resent increased Social Security taxes, fearing that when it is their turn to collect, the system will have gone broke. On the other hand, they may share common ties with new populists in a search for gaining more control in their lives, building new communities, and combining traditional values with opportunity in the future. The New Collars stand apart. They can be appealed to by right populism, progressive populism, or no populism at all.

In America of the 1980s and 1990s, three roads are imaginable: a growing trend toward the right wing, a stagnating elitist liberalism, and a new politics unlike the traditional left and right that begins to return power to average citizens. Only the last, progressive populism, offers hope for a more democratic society, a stronger economy, and the defeat of the Republican right.

In the first instance, right wing populism proposes simply more of the same anti-government "deregulation" that generates rampant greed and community dislocation. In place of finding serious solutions to the long term economic problems facing the nation, it is a politics that can only result in increasing bitterness, fear, and division among groups of the population.

Second, however, an elite liberal timidity suggests no solution. Much of conventional economic thinking by the 1980s had become closely tied to an elitist approach that sought to empower a "competent governing class" of planners and technicians. It had become detached from the lives and aspirations of ordinary citizens. Plans for aid to high tech industry or greater tax breaks and incentives for the modernization of manufacturing firms were justified in terms of "fairness" or "equity." But as Baltimore Congresswoman Barbara Mikulski pointed out, a term like "fairness" sounds abstract, failing to speak to people's sense that something is deeply wrong in America. "It doesn't generate energy. It doesn't generate passion. People can't feel it. They can't touch it. If they win it, they don't know what the hell they've got when it's all over."[18]

The new populist path offers a way to make government work again and work for the public good. The populist program is based on a very old American set of insights: for government to work there must be a solid citizenry that is educated, organized, and empowered. A sketch of the difference between progressive populist, right wing, and conventional approaches helps make the point.

Imagine three Americans in the 1980s.

THE STORY OF JOHN TURNER. John Turner's family had moved up to New Jersey from South Carolina in the late 1940s, after World War II, hopeful that the North would provide more opportunities for blacks than had the segregated South. For a time, Turner's life seemed to confirm his parents' hopes. He had graduated from high school, gotten married, landed a job in a small steel mill in the city. Turner and his wife were saving money for a small house. But the factory closed down, its products undersold by inexpensive imports made in the Far East. Turner had searched for a year for any comparable job but had found only menial work. His twelve-year-old son had begun to skip school. His marriage was in trouble. The future looked bleak.

THE STORY OF RALPH WOJTYLA. Ralph Wojtyla had spent all his life in the Polish neighborhood in his midwestern town. Sometimes it seemed insulated from the world, he thought, but the warmth of friends, extended family, parish church, and familiar neighborhood landmarks had always been more than adequate compensation. His corner grocery store had done well for two decades, and he had hoped to leave the business to his sixteen-year-old son or perhaps one of his twin daughters in junior high school. But interest rates on the loan he had taken out for repair of the building proved a greater burden than he had expected. And, most worrisome, realtors had recently been calling him late at night, warning that "the coloreds" were moving into the neighborhood, that there would soon be a rapid increase in crime, that many of his neighbors were leaving. They always ended the conversation by offering to buy him out.

THE STORY OF JANE WILDER. Jane Wilder had interviewed for a job with the insurance company on the West Coast soon after business school. Young, talented, with two years of education beyond high school, Wilder had begun work with great enthusiasm. Ten years later she felt trapped. She was at the top of the secretarial pay scale but still made less than men down in the mailroom, who mostly had only high school diplomas —but also had their own union. In her own department, she had trained several younger men for jobs that were over her classification but had not even been posted. Whatever savings she and her husband, a sales-man downtown, made seemed to be eroded by upkeep on the car, major purchases, and the costs of care for their two small children. Wilder despaired of ever being able to have a house of her own or even getting much ahead. The boss who ran her department was making advances— and one of her friends who stood up to him was now out of a job.

These are the stories of Americans in the 1980s. But they are not stories of hopeless victimization.

TURNER'S ALTERNATIVE. To John Turner, right wing populism offers little more than dog-eat-dog individualism justified by the rhetoric of the free market. If your community in the Northeast is going down hill, said President Reagan, "vote with your feet" and move to Houston where there is "more opportunity." But a milk-toast liberalism approach offers little other than growing dependency. It might provide emergency neces-sities like food stamps, welfare support, and perhaps counselling for family problems. But it fails to generate the real hope that things might substantively change for the better.

Progressive populism is the alternative: it says to Turner that his prob-lems are not individual ones. It offers models of ordinary people banding together to fight to reopen the factory if possible, to work on economic development, to refashion job programs into tools of the community. It provides an alternative to continuing dependency on government aid by recognizing the right of every American to a job sufficient for dignity and respect. It builds on innovative programs to break out of the cycle of welfare dependency, making certain that good training for jobs is available—and that the jobs will be there when the training is completed.

WOJTYLA'S ALTERNATIVE. For Ralph Wojtyla, right wing populism offers scapegoats—blacks, criminals, perhaps liberal politicians and government bureaucrats. It invokes a consoling rhetoric of family, community, and faith and the diversion of a national crusade against the communist "evil empire." But it fails to solve the problems that critically threaten the central values in his life. An elite liberalism, however, offers scarcely more—indeed, it is likely to have branded Wojtyla as "the problem," exhorting him about prejudice and fear, upholding rights of minorities to open housing or of criminals to fair trials, but defining his loyalties to neighborhood, parish, and small business as backward and parochial.

Progressive populism is the alternative. It begins, as thousands of neighborhood organizations have begun in recent years, with efforts to address the real problems of urban decay, spreading crime, and conflict between different ethnic and racial groups. It challenges unresponsive bank lenders, unscrupulous real estate interests, and demagogic politicians who seek to profit from fear and division. It builds bridges between similarly powerless communities that discover (often to common surprise) similar problems and similar concerns. On the broadest level, progressive populism teaches Wojtyla practical hope—the experience of success and cooperative action, the realization that people can do something about the problems surrounding them. And it points toward still wider connections with other communities, churches, and ethnic groups working on major social problems like bank lending practices, taxes, and interest rates.

WILDER'S ALTERNATIVE. For Jane Wilder, right wing populism counsels retreat and guilt. Concerns about child care, career advancement, treatment on the job, and similar issues are defined as simply illegitimate from a perspective that defines women's "proper place" as in the home alone. A liberal politics offers more—programs of affirmative action, support for concerns about sexual harassment, ideas of comparable worth that might bring her salary into more proper balance with the mailroom workers. But it suggests little sense of community, change in the nature of her job, or possibility of alliance with others in her workplace.

Here, too, progressive populism offers the alternative. It urges common action, through on-the-job organizations to fight for fair and equal treatment. It points toward collaboration, not simple conflict, with unionized male workers in the mailroom. It upholds notions of the dignity of work, the need for broader contact between people on the job and in the community, the right of workers to have a voice in decision making that suggests long run change in the very texture of office life. And it offers tools to fight for larger changes in public policies around issues such as day care, housing, and utility rates that offer hope of change in the nature of life off the job as well.

Progressive populism, illustrated in these stories, has spread among Middle Americans at the grass roots of America precisely because it offers an alternative to a failed conventional politics and the policies of the populist right alike. Millions of citizens have come to feel, simply, that America has been robbed of her birthright dreams and ideals and they intend to take them back. Out of such sentiments, in turn, have come organizations at local, state, and national levels through which to take action.

3. ORGANIZERS AND ACTIVISTS

The Roots of Citizen Action

We believe in democracy—in average people controlling
their lives and the right of every person to fulfill his or her
God given potential as a human being. And we are willing to take
that dream of a truly democratic America and transform it into flesh
and blood organizations of average people, who through their own
efforts, can make it into a reality for themselves and their children.

Statement from Citizen Action's founding

As a parish pastor," explained Mark Moller-Gunderson, "I had a choice of doling out fifty dollars at a time to people so they could both heat and eat, or I could work from the justice side, try to do something about the corporations and legislation that have an effect on people's lives. That's why I got involved." When Moller-Gunderson met an organizer with the citizen group Oregon Fair Share, it seemed a made-to-order opportunity for his blue collar Lutheran church in Portland. "I was familiar with community organizing because of my background in Chicago, and I was impressed with how serious they were, how they were in for the long haul." They started a chapter of the organization out of his church, and in several years Moller-Gunderson was chair of Oregon Fair Share. As a representative from Oregon, he then got involved in discussions with similar groups around the country, talking about the creation of a national organization. When Citizen Action was formed in December, 1979, Moller-Gunderson became the first national co-chair. To him, Citizen Action represented a hope for ordinary citizens across the country to participate seriously in politics. "I don't mean political in the usual sense of the word," he elaborated. "The image of cigars and smoke-filled rooms. I mean political in the sense of having an impact on the democratic process, of having the power to do something about problems like jobs and utility rates." Marie Clark, the black trade union leader (in AFSCME) from Ohio who served as Citizen Action's other first co-chair, saw the organization in similar terms. "This is the opportunity for the people to get some more clout on national issues," she explained. "It's something we've needed for a long time."[1]

Five groups were originally involved in Citizen Action: Oregon Fair Share, Massachusetts Fair Share, Illinois Public Action Council, Connecticut Citizen Action Group, and Ohio Public Interest Campaign. Others soon joined as well: New Hampshire People's Alliance, Indiana Citizen Action Coalition, Pennsylvania Public Interest Coalition (Penn PIC), Minnesota COACT, and others. Together, they began to create an infrastructure for a new populist movement nationally.

Overall the growth of Citizen Action belied the characterization of the eighties as a decade of conservatism. From its beginning as an alliance of five organizations, Citizen Action grew by mid-decade to a network of twenty state-wide organizations and organizing projects. Many of these are themselves coalitions of unions, senior groups, churches, environmentalists, community organizations, and many others. Altogether, dues are paid to Citizen Action organizations on behalf of two million people. Citizen Action's combined staff includes more than 1,500 full time organizers, door to door fund raisers, researchers, and others. Its lists of victories range from local neighborhood issues to cleanup of toxic dump sites, blocking utility rate hikes, and state and national campaigns such as reforming health care practices, working with the senior organizations to stop Social Security cuts, and fighting the decontrol of natural gas prices. The foundations of the movement remained local, in neighborhoods like Moller-Gunderson's. But its broader form took shape out of the growing realization that different communities needed to work together. It was an understanding increasingly common in the 1970s and 1980s. Such a perspective was vividly apparent in the life stories of other early co-chairs of the organization: Chuck Deppert, Cora Tucker, Doreen Del Bianco, and Lynn Cardiff.

Southern Indiana is populated partly by migrants from Kentucky who were on their way to Detroit and ran out of gas or stopped to make a phone call. "Good southern Indiana folks," Chuck Deppert describes them. People in southern Indiana grow corn and wheat and oats and soy beans in the rich, black dirt or work in factories, services, schools, and local government in the small towns that dot the region. Chuck Deppert describes himself as always "having been a little mouthy, a little pushy." But when you first meet him, Deppert strikes you as casual, friendly, slow talking, a lot like the "good southern Indiana folks" he grew up with. Deppert's father had a grocery store in the little town of Alert, Indiana, that, along with the church, was the community center. Every Saturday, farmers would gather there to sit around the potbellied stove, chewing tobacco, telling stories about "the way it really was," and eating peanuts from a hundred-pound bag he always had on hand.

Deppert became a union organizer with the Machinists in 1967, when he left his job in an electric plant in Columbus. He organized in small towns like Martinsville and larger cities like Indianapolis. "There were small towns where they actually hated unions," Deppert remembered. "But I enjoyed working with people. We'd get a campaign started, and you always made friends. You could find people to step out and be heard, take a chance, even when they knew their jobs might be on the line."

In 1977, Deppert helped get Indiana Citizen Action Coalition started. The organization began small: "in debt with me as treasurer!" he explained. But it soon became a public presence. Citizens Gas, the utility company in Indianapolis, was technically owned by the people who used its services. But its board was self-perpetuating and its meetings closed to the public. Citizen Action Coalition found out the inflated salaries of the company executives and went to a board of directors meeting. "That was the first time I ever got up in front of a large group and spoke," remembered Deppert. "I was on television. I cut my teeth on that." It wasn't the last. Deppert became a familiar public figure. The Citizen Action Coalition brought community groups, churches, labor, and others together for the first time to work on issues like plant closings, utility rates and shutoffs, and taxes. And it won a series of striking victories against some of the biggest powers in the state. By the 1980s, it had become a household word throughout the state. "Now, whenever there is a major issue, the television reporters come to our office, to ask what we think."[2]

Cora Tucker, like Deppert, has always fought for what she believes in. Daughter of a black sharecropper in Halifax County, Virginia, Tucker won a state-wide contest in the 1950s for her high school essay, "What America Means to Me." But she refused the award from the governor himself.

"They changed my essay," Tucker explained, remembering her surprise when she went up to the stage to hear it read aloud—and found that her references to segregation had been removed. "Lord, I created a stir. But it wasn't right. They weren't giving me a prize for what I wrote; they were giving me a prize for what they wanted me to say."

By the middle seventies, the racial dividing line was still rigid in much of the county. Despite being nearly 50 percent of the population, blacks constituted only 7.4 percent of the government employees and only two blacks working for the county made over ten thousand dollars a year. When the county commissioners turned down a large grant offered by the federal government for recreation programs because they would have had to follow affirmative action hiring guidelines, Tucker organized a group of black and white youth to fight back. "We brought two hundred people to the meeting, and they voted seven to zero to take the grant money. Then the next month, when there were only ten people at the meeting, they changed their minds and turned it down. The kids were so angry, after that they really began to organize."

Barred from holding public actions, Tucker and the Citizens for a Better America (CBA) decided to call a Citizens Day of Prayer. "We had it at the courthouse, because that's where everything happens to black folks. I wanted people to get so they felt like the courthouse is theirs." The idea was that, on a prayer day, "people could sing, pray, do what they wanted." They prayed for a better America. In his nearby hometown, Jerry Falwell, hearing about the day, ranted against the group for an entire week. Tucker was unfazed. Cora Tucker and CBA won.

In 1977, Tucker organized a voter registration drive to support Henry Howell, the populist gubernatorial candidate who had long sought to build an interracial coalition of blacks and working and poor whites. CBA signed up more than fifteen hundred new voters. It was the beginning of a series of victories. CBA boycotted local merchants who discriminated in hiring practices—and won wide-ranging advances for black employees. It joined with an alliance against dangerous uranium mining that brought together groups as diverse as the Chamber of Commerce, the Farm Bureau, and church groups—and won a moratorium from the state legislature. In the spring of 1982, Tucker led Citizens for a Better America into the new Virginia Action, directed by Fritz Wiecking. She became the group's first president. "There is one fundamental goal we have that is a whole lot bigger than any other problem we may face," Tucker told the group. "So many black people and white people have not worked together before and it is going to take some time for us to realize what is going on within us. But the ultimate goal is for us to organize little people to have a voice in the destiny of their lives. Everything else is secondary."[3]

Waterbury, Connecticut, is a heavily industrial town, famous for being the brass capital of the world. Doreen Del Bianco, from Waterbury's tight-knit Italian community, had a father and grandfather who were union activists and leaders; indeed her grandfather had played the key role in swinging the Italian vote to the union during a famous organizing drive of the 1930s. "But I never knew anything about that until I was an adult. In Italian culture you kind of shelter the wife and the kids. The only thing they used to talk about is that you had to get a job and put in a fair day's work." Del Bianco's family, like most Waterbury Italians, were Republicans (the product less of party ideology than of an old fight between Italians and Irish in the city) and fearful of those who seemed different. "I was a housewife, and blamed all my troubles on blacks, Puerto Ricans, and other victims," she describes. But when she helped her husband open a small restaurant, she was enraged at the skyrocketing utility bills and answered the invitation of a local organizer to come to a meeting sponsored by Waterbury Citizen Action Group. She saw the group win on the issue and found new confidence to join with neighbors on other issues.

Powerful, articulate, dynamic, Del Bianco quickly became a leader. In her early twenties, she chaired a meeting of thirteen hundred people in Waterbury, protesting reassessments of property taxes. The city wanted to raise taxes on residential homes by hundreds of dollars and simultaneously decrease taxes on the utility and other corporations by tens of thousands of dollars. As a result of the meeting and Connecticut Citizen Action Group's subsequent campaign, middle income homeowners got tax relief. And Del Bianco found herself changing from the new experiences of empowerment and the new relationships alike. "I woke up one day and realized it was more than utilities. When you're in a meeting and there are blacks and Puerto Ricans and elderly and women and you talk with them, your stereotypes change." In 1982, Del Bianco, by then well known throughout the community, was elected to the state legislature as a spokeswoman for the state-wide Connecticut Citizen Action Group.[4]

Like Del Bianco, Lynn Cardiff, when she was growing up in California, thought little about social activism of any sort. "In fact, I didn't think anything about politics at all until I was thirty-two or thirty-three," Cardiff recalls. She had grown up in Fresno, California, and had led what she remembers as a "normal middle class life," concerned with friends, school, dates, and the like. After briefly attending college, Cardiff got married "to a man who would take care of me and tell me what to do." They soon had two children. When her husband, a salesman of agricultural chemicals, got a job in Oregon, they moved to the state capital of Salem. But when she went back to college, began learning about scientific and environmental issues, and raised tentative questions about the effects of chemicals on the environment, increasing tension developed in the marriage. Eventually divorced and a single parent, she also became a dynamic teacher. When someone from a neighborhood citizen organization called Oregon Fair Share knocked at her door in

1978, Cardiff became a leader. Fair Share, designed by its founding director, Kim Clerc, and others to address a wide range of neighborhood and consumer issues, produced results. Cardiff helped lead the organization in fights ranging from community concerns to toxic hazards across the state. Once she negotiated, alone, with the governor's top aides. "When I began, I was petrified to go in front of a public official and say anything. But I learned if you go in numbers, they're scared to death, too." Such active involvement, moreover, changed her understanding of the relation between public officials and the people, in the process reviving older ideas. "People say, 'You can't fight city hall. You can't do anything about it.' But to me, what it means to be an American is having control over your government. That's what we're about. That's democracy." On a more personal level, Oregon Fair Share and Citizen Action have given Cardiff a new understanding of herself. "It was like finding my identity and my voice," recounts Cardiff. "Fair Share was my way of doing something about what I believed in. It became a way of life." [5]

The broad conception of coalition on which leaders like Deppert, Tucker, Del Bianco, and Cardiff reflected had its roots in the experiences of local citizens who had often won important local victories that had given them a sense that you *can* fight city hall. Through such experience, they had also come to see the need for unified, common action in the face of changing conditions and growing concentrations of power.

Bob Hudek, field director of Citizen Action, has seen a dramatic change over the years from a focus on local officials and decision makers to a widespread understanding of the need for larger alliances in order to win. "You take a local dump-site activist who's been concerned about kids being poisoned by toxic waste. They go to the bureaucracy and get a runaround. Then people understand that the only way this sort of problem is really going to be solved is if they have more power and join with others to get the government to clamp down on polluters and establish a cleanup fund." By the time of the founding of Citizen Action, organizers like Hudek had many years of experience putting coalitions and alliances together. The need for broader networks and alliances to advance the power of ordinary citizens against special interests, concentrated wealth, and unresponsive bureaucracies was the central lesson that organizers learned from the sixties and sought to put into practice in the seventies.[6]

Bill Thompson, a poet, had been a black leader in the 1960s and early 1970s. He looked for a new way to organize as the times changed. "We figured it was time to understand the American people, white, black, what have you, and speak to their ear rather than to talk at them." Thompson had become disillusioned with the rhetorical posturing of much of sixties-style activism. "You have to calculate and organize more effectively, build a broader base using different tactics." So he became a major organizer for a new state-wide group called Massachusetts Fair Share, which sought to bring people together across the lines of bitter racial division that had opened in the wake of the Boston busing crisis. He organized chapters of Fair Share in black areas like Roxbury. "No matter where they get it, if people who have the experience of struggling, it's healthy. Any kind of situation, mothers for child care or whatever, that makes people realize that institutions are not functioning well, that their future is not tied into how many degrees their son or daughter can get, is an education."[7]

Thompson was part of a new generation of organizers, many veterans of sixties protests, for whom grass roots work had become a career. They developed their skills and strategic thinking as a part of a broader dialogue. In the early seventies, new centers for training citizen organizers and leaders developed across the country, with names like the Industrial Areas Foundation, the National Training and Information Center, Organize Training Center, and the Midwest Academy.

Heather Booth was born near Jackson, Mississippi, where her father was stationed with the army during World War II. After the war, her family moved to Brooklyn, New York, where she grew up in a mixed ethnic neighborhood. In the summer of 1964, at the height of the Civil Rights Movement, Booth returned to her birth state of Mississippi to help register blacks to vote. Later, in Chicago during the fall of 1967, she helped organize one of the first organizations of the new women's movement in the country and for several years organized women in

Chicago communities around issues like child care. Out of such diverse experiences she decided to be a teacher of the sorts of lessons taught in civil rights "freedom schools." Such schools, where black youngsters acquired literacy and learned to be proud of black history, were also organizing centers where people heard stories about other communities around the country and across the ocean that were similarly fighting for freedom and developing practical skills of organizing. In 1973, Booth founded the Midwest Academy in part as heir to the freedom school tradition.

The Midwest Academy began offering training sessions for organizers from groups as diverse as local neighborhood organizations, Massachusetts Fair Share, religious organizations, trade unions, the National Organization for Women, and the Nuclear Freeze. The Academy taught a variety of nuts and bolts organizing skills like running meetings, raising money, doing research, and planning a public event. From the beginning, it was also informed with a broader vision. It became a place to discuss broad strategies and build a network of similarly committed activists.

The setting for grass roots organizing had begun to change dramatically by the 1970s. Many organizations of poor people, the young, and others that had had considerable momentum in the 1960s climate of social activism faced new obstacles in a situation of fiscal austerity, intransigent business opposition, and a growing right wing. Moreover, sixties protests, for all their strength and appeal, had left a legacy of often bitter divisions between groups—white ethnics and blacks, welfare recipients and middle income taxpayers, hardhats and environmentalists, the young and the old. At the same time, the changing climate had produced a growing activism among many "Middle American" groups that sixties protests had not touched and brought to the forefront a number of populist economic issues, from taxes to utility rates, which offered new possibilities for broader alliances.

Chicago, the "windy city" celebrated by Carl Sandburg, was an ideal location for a new approach. Its industrial, blue collar, and ethnic neighborhoods had seen generations of organizing by pioneers in grass roots democratic action. Saul Alinsky, the dean of the tradition, had started there with the Back of the Yards Organization in the 1930s. Chicago had proved training ground for later, legendary figures in the craft of organizing, from Father John Egan and Nicholas Von Hoffman to Gale Cincotta, Ed Chambers, Shel Trapp, Peter Martinez, Tom Gaudette, Richard Harmon, Ernie Cortes, Stan Holt, John Baumann, and many others. In the early 1970s, the Midwest Academy worked alongside the newly formed Citizen Action Program (CAP) in Chicago, a group that Saul Alinsky's training center, the Industrial Areas Foundation, had organized in 1970 as the first major attempt to build metropolitan organization, bringing together a wide range of communities across lines of earlier division. Booth's husband, Paul Booth, a former leader of the student movement, was co-chair of CAP with Father Lenard Dubi. CAP combined the spirit of sixties activism with a community organizing approach to work on problems like pollution and taxes and bank lending practices that appealed to many middle income communities in the city. It suggested the need for new coalitions that were not divided by race or ethnicity or class. Its roots continued to be in particular neighborhoods, but such communities sent representatives to a city-wide steering committee that determined issues of broad appeal and importance. The curriculum director of the Academy, Steve Max, had long urged such an approach within the sixties student movement and later had sought to build ties between unions and community groups. He knew from years of experience that such populist approaches had been the key to the success of past democratic movements. With wry humor, Max would tell of the rich histories of such earlier movements in America, largely unknown by current activists.

Then, in 1976, Karen Thomas came on staff as the Midwest Academy's second director. Thomas had been organizer of a new organization in California, the Citizen Action League, which was one of the first attempts to put such a broad coalition approach to work on a state-wide basis. She later became associate director of Citizen Action.

According to the Academy, three key principles were at the heart of "direct action organizing" that builds ongoing citizen groups. As the basic strategy book of the Academy put it:

> Direct Action organizing aims to win real and immediate improvements in people's lives. Whether the improvement is ending

job discrimination or lowering utility rates, Direct Action organizing attempts to win it for large numbers of people rather than helping a person with an individual problem.

Direct Action organizing gives people a sense of their own real power. In this way, membership feels the sense of accomplishment that is necessary to continue and to win further victories.

Direct Action organizing attempts to alter the relations of power between people's organizations and their real enemies. The enemies are often unresponsive politicians, tax assessors, utilities, landlords, government agencies, large corporations, or banks. The relations of power are altered by building permanent, ongoing institutions of the people.

The final point, "changing the relations of power" in the society, was also seen as a new direction that moved beyond the single-constituency focus of activism in the sixties toward a more active, inclusive understanding of "making democracy work." The broad strategy appropriate to the seventies, in the Academy's view, was to unite groups that had been antagonistic, including whites, blacks, Hispanics, the poor and the middle class, environmentalists, union members, and farmers. "Often people were pitted against each other," Steve Max explained. "The consumer against the worker, the person who breathed dirty air against the person who produced it. We are cutting across economic, ethnic and racial lines by concentrating on issues that affect the lives of all these groups." In the face of intractable opponents and a deteriorating economic environment, organizing required a "majority perspective." "The issues raised and the demands made have to be ones which *most* people will support, if not actively work for."[8]

The Midwest Academy's lessons in organizing and vision provided new perspectives for many coming out of sixties student activism who sought new ways of putting their ideals to work for the longer term. "It was like a revelation," explained Ellen Cassedy, a graduate of the Midwest Academy and talented organizer who helped establish one of the first groups of working women, 9 to 5, in Boston, from which the movie title and song eventually derived. "For the first time I thought seriously about how to listen to what secretaries in my office were interested in, and the need to build an organization that would be based on gaining people a voice. It opened up a whole new way of thinking."[9]

The Academy adapted such lessons to the evolving political and social climate in the country as well. In 1977 and 1978, it proved a key force in building working relations between state-wide citizen groups around the country. As a place for broad strategic thinking as well as training in the nuts and bolts of organizing, the Academy became a major reference point for hundreds and then thousands of organizers. Its Annual Retreat, begun in 1974, has turned into a massive event that is part cultural festival, part educational conference, and part forum for strategic and political discussions for the new populism.

The Academy and similar institutions began to form strategic centers for new populist organizing. A few foundations and donors agreed strongly with the need for grass roots organizations of ordinary citizens that would build power on an ongoing basis. They began to fund the nonpartisan, educational work of such efforts. Among these were: A Territory Resource, Arca Foundation, Beldon Fund, Bydale, the Campaign for Human Development, Discount Foundation, J. C. Penney Foundation, New World Foundation, Norman Foundation, Philadelphia Foundation, Rockefeller Family Associates, Samuel Rubin Foundation, Shalan Foundation, Stern Family Fund, Sunflower Foundation, Veatch/ North Shore Unitarian Church Program, Villers Foundation, the Youth Project, and many others. With such resources in place, a growing number of organizers and leaders experimented with ways to put new populist ideas into practice.

In Illinois, Robert Creamer, a former divinity school student who had gone to work with the Citizen Action Program, organized a board of community and institutional representatives in 1975 to explore the possibilities of forming a state-wide organization called Illinois Public Action Council, (IPAC). He hired Jackie Kendall, who had previously been a community leader in suburban Chicago and a main figure in the national meat boycott in the early 1970s, as one of the organizers for the new group. "At first I couldn't believe we were going to do it; I was real skeptical that we'd be able to unite people across the state and win,"

Kendall remembers. "We went around the state trying to find who was out there and what they were interested in." She found people like Marie Clay, a senior citizen leader with the group Metro Seniors in Action in Chicago, who saw the opportunity through Illinois Public Action to unite with other senior citizens around the state, and Joe Ruiz, whose community organizing efforts in the polyglot, ethnically diverse areas of the southeast side of Chicago had convinced him that new alliances were possible. "What's made us stronger in striving for what we want is we have blacks, latinos, whites. It's all mixed." explained Ruiz. "Everybody now had come together and sat down in a chair instead of feuding. We've finally realized that the only way to solve these problems is not separating each individual race." [10]

Kendall and other organizers discovered that groups that had been doubtful about the value of common work were quickly convinced. "We actually began winning things at the state level on taxes, utility rates, and other issues," she remembered. "And it was fun; it was exciting. People really enjoyed working with others from all over the state. I remember one conference early on. I came walking by and saw a black community leader from Chicago sitting in the middle of a group of white farmers. She was holding forth. I went, 'Oh, my God, what are they talking about?' It turned out that she grew up on a farm in Mississippi. They were all having a discussion about growing different crops." [11]

Organizations like Oregon Fair Share, Massachusetts Fair Share, and Illinois Public Action Council grew because they won concrete victories and met people's desire to build bonds with neighbors and find new dignity. When Jackie Kendall became director of the Midwest Academy in 1982, she brought a wealth of concrete coalition-building experience to the practice of organizer training. The effort to build coalitions was also informed by sophisticated analysis.

Ira Arlook, a civil rights and student activist in the 1960s, had settled in Cleveland, Ohio. He was a key figure in developing a longer range strategy for putting the analysis and skills of sixties movement activists to work in ways that would appeal to a broad cross section of the population. "I was always skeptical about the traditional community organizers' view of how people's minds developed," he recounted. "The idea that you first had to work on stop signs and then, incrementally, people's ideas would broaden never was true in my opinion. I always thought people are capable of other things—understanding the need for broader organization, the need for electoral politics. What we had to do was combine the view that the basic problems America faced were based on the structure and behavior of giant corporations with concerns that had immediate effect in people's daily lives." Arlook and others were convinced that the mobility of industry was proving increasingly devastating in states like Ohio, as corporations moved to the South and Southwest or overseas in search of higher profits. Plant closings left in their wake "not only a dramatic loss of employment, but also a loss of tax base, the destruction of families, the ripping apart of communities' fabric. It aggravated all the tensions that already existed and set people against each other."

Arlook approached labor unions, which had an immediate and obvious self-interest in addressing the problem of plant closings, and found an enthusiastic response to ideas for developing some program that would begin to address the issues. "But we felt that unless the issue was seen as more than a labor question it wouldn't be enough. It was really a public interest question that meant senior citizens should be concerned, traditional community organizations should be concerned, religious congregations, even many small businesspeople." In Ohio in 1975, Arlook and others formed the Ohio Public Interest Campaign, or OPIC, as a coalition of existing organizations to work on issues like plant closings and taxes. Its structure was unlike Massachusetts Fair Share and other groups, which had a base of chapter members. Involving people from existing organizations had advantages. "It meant people forming the committees of OPIC were very experienced. They knew what it meant to organize a base, they had skills, they understood the usefulness of a coalition." OPIC was able to assure neighborhoods and trade unions that they could join together on common concerns and not surrender autonomy. Most important, it created a means for articulating and acting on a common vision: "Our vision was to encroach on the power of the major corporations and to advance popular power, to counter the narrow private interest with the public interest." With victories on issues that ranged from taxes to plant closings, it soon proved possible to do so.[12]

By the mid-seventies, informal networks of friendship and contact had begun to generate discussion of the need for broader national alliances. Nationally, moreover, those involved in public interest campaigns of the sort pioneered by Ralph Nader were increasingly interested in working with local and state groups. Bob Brandon, public interest advocate and author of the book *Tax Politics*, which had championed many of the issues that state-wide citizen groups were concerned about, had seen a significant, growing realization in the Washington public interest community. "The business interests were getting more and more entrenched in Washington. You could see the corporate lobbying and how it could turn around even good legislators. So more and more people in Washington realized they had to have a base of support on local levels for public interest issues."[13]

Within the mainstream of progressive reform organizations, two leaders, William Winpisinger of the Machinists union and William Hutton of the National Council of Senior Citizens, proved key figures in translating such insights into ongoing reality. Winpisinger had long believed that the labor movement could be revitalized through new forms of alliance and new experiments in grass roots activism. Feisty, blunt, indefatigable in carrying out his commitments, Winpisinger (or "Wimpy" as he is affectionately known) had a new opportunity to try out his ideas when he assumed the presidency of the union in 1976 and became a member of the AFL-CIO executive committee. Meeting with Brandon, Heather Booth, and others from the networks of citizen groups, he determined to forge a new sort of coalition.

Winpisinger not only put his prestige and reputation on the line, he committed his union's resources as well. Local Machinist lodges followed his lead and started to work with citizen organizations on many issues. He had the vision to see that meeting the challenge of new times required that unions reach out beyond the confines of the work place to deal with the needs of their members and their neighbors as consumers, tax payers, homeowners, and parents and in many other ways. Much of the credit for the successes of the Citizen Action organizations is due to his efforts.

Bill Hutton had a similar dream. For years he had worked to create a massive, activist organization of senior citizens. Hutton was convinced that those who had "retired" from paid work needed to organize both to represent their own self-interests and to mobilize their invaluable resources of experience, energy, and talent in addressing the nation's problems. Like Winpisinger, Hutton believed in broader alliances to realize his hopes. He was determined to counter the growing fragmentation of society into "interest groups" and isolated communities. He wanted to see lasting ties between seniors and the young, communities, labor unions, consumers, and every other segment of America. Bill Hutton brought years of organizing experience to the effort. A master of the style of oratory so rarely practiced these days, he travelled the country speaking to senior and citizen groups about their common stake in the energy issue.

Through the efforts of Winpisinger, Hutton, and many others, in April, 1978, representatives of more than seventy citizen and community groups, labor unions, senior citizen efforts, farm organizations, and low income organizing projects founded the Citizen Labor Energy Coalition, or CLEC. Its founding purpose declared the intention to create "a permanent coalition dedicated to building a nation-wide grassroots organization that would reduce the power of the energy industry over our economy and government." The principles of the group fleshed out the intention:

1. Energy prices must be just, reasonable, and affordable for all consumers.
2. Energy policies must promote economic health through the preservation and creation of jobs.
3. The concentrated economic power in the energy industry must be broken up.
4. Energy must be safe and national energy policies must be sensitive to the health and welfare of all Americans.

William Winpisinger was chosen CLEC president. William Hutton became the secretary-treasurer. "It was unique," said Hutton. "We've been looking for a way to build a coalition where each can strengthen the other. Each has something to contribute. We all have a stake in building a better country. Seniors have been contributing all our lives." The board of directors consisted of representatives of different groups, carefully balanced to consist of roughly one third community organizations, one third unions, and one third national groups like seniors and environmentalists.[14]

The national structure was intended to balance autonomy of the organizational affiliates with strong national leadership and common initiatives around key issues. It was often not simple. Don Wiener, former organizing co-director of CLEC, remembered a number of continuing problems. "Many groups we worked with had little experience working together in coalitions, and the terms of joint work had to be constantly renegotiated." Moreover, the balance between wide local autonomy and coordinated national action was complex and difficult. "How to set priorities, find agreement on common tactics, agree to disagree about other issues—all of these questions kept coming up." Yet the sense that the Coalition was joined together by a common strategy and a common sense of objectives also meant that there was on balance "surprisingly little conflict" overall. And on state levels where the Coalition took on life, it created new forums for joint work and relationships.[15]

In Iowa, a state where no group like Massachusetts Fair Share or Illinois Public Action existed, Tami Odell, a young, dynamic woman not long out of college, had been doing community organizing in Sioux City. She heard that an organizing meeting for CLEC was going to be held in Des Moines, in the fall of 1978; she decided to go. "There were seven people sitting around a table drinking beer," Odell remembered. "I call it beer diplomacy. Bill Fenton from the Machinists, Chuck Gifford from the Auto Workers, Mable and Earl Reed from the State Council of Senior Citizens, Don Rowan from the State Federation. A fellow named Cliff Humphrey from South Central Retirees, a man named Henry Pontias who'd organized his own group called Seniors United for Action. People said, 'We've got to move ahead on this.' We talked about utility shutoffs, and how poor people needed help. Seniors saw it as a way to build their own organizations. Labor saw it as a way to help their members. At the same time, I think everybody thought, 'This isn't really going to work.' But they said, 'Why don't you take care of it, Tami. We're too busy.'"

Odell became the first staff director of Iowa CLEC, full time in 1979, when the group got a grant from the Campaign for Human Development, the Catholic social justice funding agency. It did work, in large measure, because of Odell's energy and enthusiasm. "CLEC was a brilliant idea," Odell recounted. "It brought together major players that I wouldn't ordinarily have had access to—the State Council of Senior Citizens, poor people's groups, community organizations, and unions like the United Auto Workers." The coalition quickly grew from six initial groups to more than fifty. Odell encouraged friendly competition between different groups in the coalition when they had a demonstration or a day of lobbying at the state capitol: "Who could bring the buses, who got to pay, who got the credit, who could turn out more."

CLEC also provided a unique opportunity for groups to make contact. In 1983 Iowa CLEC decided to become an ongoing citizen organization, the Iowa Citizen Action Network, which then affiliated with Citizen Action.[16]

Citizen Action developed a three-part strategy. It sought to build local and state-wide organizations through which citizens could gain power on a continuing basis. It mobilized people in campaigns around deeply felt economic and quality issues. Finally, it developed an electoral dimension that supported carefully selected candidates for office. Each element was seen as essential in building foundations for a longer term political movement. Issue campaigns were the "energy source" for achieving organizational development, solidifying members' commitments, recruiting new members and organizations, developing skills. Election campaigns had been long suspect among community organizations for the potential risks involved of losing allies or getting too tied to politicians' careers. But when undertaken carefully, such campaigns turned out, as we will see in Chapter Eight, to provide key tests of the breadth of organizational support and key ways for citizens to gain representation "within the system," while they also pressured from outside.

In Wisconsin, Republican Governor Richard Dreyfus, famous for wearing a red vest, found his nickname used for unanticipated purposes. On March 16, 1982, hundreds of members of Wisconsin Citizen Labor Energy Coalition marched on the capitol in Madison wearing black vests with messages that read, "Out of the Red—Tax Big Oil!" The lobbying capped a two-year effort to pass a tax on the oil companies' excessive profits. Faced with a choice between cuts in state services and a sales tax, the governor reversed his stand and supported the oil company tax. The victory taught the possibilities of ongoing organization, and the coalition became the Wisconsin Action Coalition, an affiliate of Citizen Action. "Working together we can curb the special interests which control our economy," explained Richard Presser, business representative of the Machinists union at the founding convention. "We can build Citizen Power."

WAC found imaginative tools for building such power. Massive layoffs had hit the area around Milwaukee. To help the unemployed and add to its own strength, the organization adopted a program created by Al Levie, an unemployed machinist who had gotten sponsorship of the labor council in nearby Waukesha. The idea was for the unemployed to help themselves and other laid off workers by going to stores and winning agreements for discounts on purchases. "We set up nine sites where the unemployed could go, fill out a form and get a discount card," Levie described. "We signed up ninety-five hundred in the first year. And we got agreement from all sorts of merchants."

The program turned out to mean more than dollars and cents. "People working to help themselves meant a new sense of dignity and respect from the fact that they're working with people in the same boat," Levie explained. "It reinforced the sense it's not just your fault as an individual."

The merchant discount program was only the first step. The unemployed, many of whom had lost their cars, then fought for and won a 50 percent discount on local buses. Along with other groups in WAC they moved into campaigns that ranged from plant closing legislation and health insurance to fighting mortgage foreclosures.

The discount program aided WAC as a whole, building strong ties with labor unions, churches, and community groups that wanted to do something about the problem of unemployment and creating an active, strong, and interracial base of members among those who had suffered layoffs. "Even when people go back to work, they continue to be active in WAC in their parish or union local," said Jeff Eagan, WAC's staff director.[17]

In other states like Washington, issues also built the organization. In

Seattle, Max Rossman, a retired education director for AFSCME, found in Fair Share (the state Citizen Action affiliate) a strong ally when senior citizens throughout the city took on Slade Gorton, the U.S. senator who planned to cut Social Security benefits in 1985. "Out of that fight we developed a working relationship between Fair Share and the National Council of Senior Citizens," Rossman related. "We realized we had common goals."[18]

Nationally, Citizen Action faced a number of challenges and difficulties in building a credible network of groups and coalitions that could mount serious opposition to right wing and corporate plans. As CLEC had discovered, there were no simple answers to the problems of building a strong national presence while preserving wide latitude for independent action and organizing in local and state groups. Compared with the lavish resources of the New Right, funding for Citizen Action's national staff and operations was scant indeed. When the organization developed a national structure with two staff co-directors, Heather Booth and Ira Arlook, it found it had to spend much time in fundraising efforts that diverted energy and attention from other work like coalition building and longer range development of strategy. Funding is still difficult. The groups are often understaffed, and the remarkably talented staff is relatively low paid. "We joke that we earn about one-third of what we might in the for-profit world," says Rochelle Davis, who manages the finances and administration for national Citizen Action. Some of the groups' funding is precarious. Many have gone through difficult transitions. But they keep growing as word of their success spreads.[19]

As the network of groups associated with Citizen Action expanded, it found it faced the complex and often difficult challenge of becoming racially and culturally representative. But, like fundraising and issues of internal organizational democracy and coordination, Citizen Action has responded to the need with energy. Si Kahn, executive director of Grassroots Leadership and southern co-ordinator for Citizen Action, believes that the organization's commitment to affirmative action at every level of leadership and staff reflects in part a crucial ability to be self-critical. "There's a very strong sense in Citizen Action that you are what you eat," he explains. "You can't move toward a democratic society by less than democratic means, with the full understanding that we're all imperfect. If you want to succeed, you have to recognize where political strength lies. The way we can win is by bringing together the major dispossessed and powerless groups in our society. You can't build a progressive movement, for instance, unless women are central." Growing numbers of women staff directors began to change the traditional definition of what an "organizer" was like. "All the way back to union organizing in the 1930s there was an idea of an organizer as a kind of 'John Wayne, Have Gun Will Travel' tough guy. We're in the middle of a process toward another perspective which is much healthier."[20]

Sandra McArthur, staff director of Pennsylvania Public Interest Coalition, or Penn PIC, in Philadelphia, who had been a leader of black student politics in college, also has observed changes since she began as an organizer for New Jersey Citizen Action. "In New Jersey when I came on staff, it helped to bring the issue of multiracial organizing into focus," she explained. McArthur sees the emergence of a multiracial organization and movement as a long term process, requiring a recognition of the need for diverse forms of organizing. "There need to be organizations in the black community that address our own particular agenda of issues," she explains. "And there also need to be places like Penn PIC where we can come together with other communities, talk to each other, find what we have in common, and start working on it."[21]

Leaders like Winpisinger, Hutton, Moller-Gunderson, Cardiff, Deppert, Tucker, and Del Bianco and organizers like Thomas, Creamer, Kendall, Kahn, McArthur, and Arlook embodied the revival of democratic populism in the 1970s and 1980s. Such a growing social force had many faces and voices, far beyond the networks of Citizen Labor Energy Coalition and Citizen Action alone. It could be seen in the thousands of community organizations that formed in American neighborhoods— and in the new spirit of social concern and social involvement in America's churches and synagogues. The message of grass roots, democratic empowerment emerged in parent associations working on problems of schools, in organizations of college students getting active in surrounding communities, in networks of peace organizations working to stop military interventions in the Third World and to reverse the deadly spiral of the nuclear arms race. It was visible in working women's groups, in activist environmental organizations, in self-help groups, and in a myriad of other settings.

Citizen Action both reflected and helped shape such ferment. There was nothing settled or secure about citizen groups in the rapidly changing environment of the early 1980s: many groups' financial base and coalitional structures remained fragile. Some ended, reformed, began again.

The social force represented by the new grass roots activism has just begun to emerge. Like the first Populists, who went from farm to farm in the 1880s and 1890s, modern populism had also developed a door to door technique, called "the canvass." The canvass has become a way to communicate the possibilities for democratic empowerment in a society where such hopes have long been declining.

4. CARRYING A MESSAGE

We are walking, we are walking . . . through the country
Every door opens a door, every door opens a door . . . to the future.

Canvasser song by Si Kahn

Despite carefully tended lawns and cultivated, well-kept flower gardens, the steady rain and chill night air made the suburban neighborhood in North St. Paul, Minnesota, seem bleak. But Linda Haese, at twenty-one already a field manager of canvass teams for Citizen Action, was unruffled. As members of her canvass team got out of the car to begin door knocking in their designated areas, Haese got out with them and spoke privately, intensely, about how they are going to communicate the issues in this neighborhood and meet or exceed their nightly quota of raising ninety dollars in contributions and involving people in the organization. "Everyone needs a little inspiration," she said later. "I remind them how important their day to day work is and we set the nightly goal." When Haese parked and began her own route, she decided to do something about the rain. "We'll have to canvass for an umbrella," she explained.

Haese, her short blond hair already wet, knocked loudly on the door of the small red brick house. An elderly woman opened it a crack. "What do you want?" she asked.

"Hi, my name is Linda. We're with the citizen organization Minnesota COACT." She said that COACT worked with groups around the country.

"We're the organization that blocked the gas companies from doubling our gas bills last year." Haese, holding out her clipboard with a petition in support of COACT's efforts, briefly explained the organization's current efforts. "I don't think I'm interested; it won't do any good," the woman said softly, eyes downcast.

Haese crouched until she met the woman's eyes. Her pose radiated energy and confidence. In a few sentences she argued back. "The only way to win is to fight back. Why don't you join with your neighbors?" She pointed to the signatures on the petition and explained at greater length that COACT had indeed succeeded in past fights with the big oil companies. The woman offered a contribution.

"We also need you to write a letter to your congressman," said Haese. A few minutes later, contribution, signature, and umbrella borrowed for the evening in hand, Haese explained more why she loves the work. "Where else can someone like me, at my age and with my relative inexperience, have the level of responsibility that I now do in my job as a field manager? In the business world, I'd have to work years to make this kind of career step. If you've got it—the skills, the commitment to social justice, and the enthusiasm for the work—you can go a long way." Haese had travelled widely around the country to different Citizen Action organizations such as COACT. She had gotten, she said, "an amazing political education." And everywhere she felt that the organization was "like her family." Memories of her working class family background, it turned out, were central to Haese's motivation. "You never can give up, when you talk to someone at the door," she said, walking down the street. "I feel like I'm talking to my parents, trying to convince them not to give up. People have to get involved. I'm bringing the citizen movement to every door I knock on." She glowed with the memories of people she had met. "Last night, an old man told me when I left, 'I'm with you all the way. Go get them.' He was talking about COACT. But he was also talking about me." [1]

Staff of Citizen Action and allied democratic populist organizations now every week, night after night (five days a week), knock on the doors of about fifty thousand homes. Each canvasser visits forty homes a night, two hundred a week. Over a month's time, the cumulative canvass reaches more than a million American families. In a year, canvassers contact twelve million. In states where canvass operations have been in existence for a number of years, they have given organizations like Massachusetts Fair Share, Ohio Public Interest Campaign, and Illinois Public Action a remarkable level of public recognition; Massachusetts Fair Share is known by upward of 80 percent of the general public in the state.[2] The canvass brings information about issue organizing campaigns to the general public, identifies citizens who wish to be directly involved in such efforts, raises money, serves as a voter education and mobilization instrument during elections, and functions as a vast dialogue with millions of Americans about particular issues and the broader possibility of democracy itself.

The canvass was developed in the early 1970s first as a new sort of fundraising technique—"selling social change door to door, the way you sell encyclopedias," as Marc Anderson, its creator, remembers. "It was supposed to be a reliable source of capital for organizing. Within a year it had proved that it was." The canvass was especially attractive as a method of providing a source of funds for citizen organizations that was independent of government, foundations, and other large institutions. Canvass efforts face external problems, like skeptical local governments. They often battle against restrictive solicitation laws until they have established their legitimacy and professionalism. (Responsible canvass operations register all names of canvassers with local police departments and issue clear credentials.) And they have to develop internal methods of monitoring quality of work, goal setting, and minimum standards of pay in order to sustain such operations for any length of time.[3]

As the canvass evolved as a means of fundraising, initially intended only to support the actual work of "organizing," citizen activists increasingly came to value it as a remarkably flexible and effective two-way method of communication in its own right.

Canvasses constantly convey to the public information about the issues that state organizations and the national organization are working on. They also fathom the public's mood and sometimes help determine the potential of issues that organizations are considering. Canvasses now sign up a large at-large membership in citizen groups, which get a regular newsletter and are regularly recontacted by phone. They also are used to identify those who wish to be more involved—from participating in legislative phone trees that can be activated to put pressure on politicians, to attending public events, to becoming active participants in organizational matters. Follow-up telephone canvasses allow regular contact with thousands of citizens. During election seasons, the canvass has increasingly been used to collect masses of demographic and political information about voters, to target political constituencies, to identify volunteers, to get out the vote.

The canvass has developed into a sophisticated tool for large scale issue and political campaigns. People in many states come to expect contact with a canvasser every year and often convey at the door their evaluations and opinions of the organization's work. In sum, it is a kind of vast dialogue with the public, the frontline communications technique of the new populism.[4]

The canvass consists, essentially, of a one-on-one contact with a straightforward message of empowerment. As Larry Marx, a leader in the canvass puts it, "We interrupt people's normal realities and ask for their support. But the basic message is that people don't have to just take it. We're not helpless victims. We can control our own lives."[5]

Haese's team of seven that night is diverse. If, after an initial training period, the canvassers continue to fulfill regularly their quota of contributions and do well at involving people, they can stay on, earning a modest income and a bonus that represents a portion of any money raised above the quota. A few on the team had been at it for a number of months; most were fairly new—students working for the summer. Canvassing is challenging work that requires energy and discipline. Some would continue, perhaps travelling to other cities around the country, perhaps moving to a new city to help open a new canvass office. Even those who leave after a short while typically find the experience politically motivating and useful.

Haese asked them to explain why they were canvassing. Heidi Minwegen, twenty-seven, a single mother who had previously worked for the Army's Defense Language Institute in California, explains that she can't stand the passivity she sees around her. "People are so ready to lay down and die. We might as well be pawns for corporations and the government. I want to see everyone meet at least one live person who will tell them, 'Go out in the street and yell if you do nothing else.'" Others range from Gary, a forty-year-old beekeeper, who says he has "been political for many years" and sees the canvass as a new method of political education, to Bob, a young divinity school student, who believes the canvass "helps create contacts in a society where there aren't very many."[6]

Back at the COACT office late that night, the scene resembles the purposeful jumble of a political campaign headquarters. On one wall are maps of Twin City neighborhoods; on another, political posters: of Ronald Reagan in a cowboy suit, with the caption, "Bedtime for Brezhnev"; of the Catholic social justice group Campaign for Human Development with the words "If you want peace work for justice"; of the legendary labor activist Mother Jones with her quote "Pray for the Dead. Fight Like Hell for the Living"; of the social stratification of the United States. Canvassers from different teams that have worked in several neighborhoods in Minneapolis and St. Paul, the Twin Cities, come back in and tally up their amounts raised and support letters generated (the organization has been asking for letters on the utility issue). They fill out cards on each person who has contributed or expressed support, recording brief impressions, any particular concerns, and a rating of how likely the person is to get involved in different sorts of activities.[7]

As a whole, the canvassers are even more diverse than Haese's team. There are several foreign students (from Nigeria, the Middle East, Cameroon); young people recently off farms in the Midwest; a black organizer from inner city Chicago neighborhoods; a long time trade union member; a former nurse who has made a career change; an elderly political activist who is putting his experience to work in a new way. Twenty-five or so canvassers had gone out altogether, and, on average, they had exceeded their objectives despite the rain.

Staff who stay on often build careers in the canvassing field. By taking on increasing levels of responsibility in the directing of a canvass office and by attending training sessions (which cover topics such as how to develop more leadership skills, how to function as a political leader as well as a staff supervisor), canvassers can qualify for promotions, first to field manager, then to canvass director.

George Knotek, over thirty and director of the canvass for Minnesota COACT, has decided to plant his roots in this organizing with the canvass. Raised in a devoutly Catholic family that was deeply involved in community activities in Downer's Grove, Illinois, Knotek has lived in the Twin Cities for ten years. Knotek is intimately acquainted with Twin Cities neighborhoods and believes that canvass directors in organizations like COACT need to have roots in a place, raise families, become involved in local politics. "Canvassers need connections with both a national and the local community," he explains, describing the national canvass network directed by the Citizen Labor Energy Coalition that works with state groups like COACT. "If you stay in the canvass for long, you travel around the country, working in another office—crosstraining is what we call it. Early in your career you see first hand that this really is a national movement. You go to an office in State College, Pennsylvania [with the organization Penn PIC], for example. There you might meet canvassers from San Jose [CED], Silver Spring [Maryland Citizen Action Coalition], and Cedar Rapids [Iowa Citizen Action Network]." In fact, it is this fabric of canvassers crisscrossing the country, building up existing offices, opening new ones that provided much of the foundation to build the national Citizen Action.[8]

While seeing the national vision as important, Knotek views connecting locally as equally needed. Indeed, for Knotek, such connection is ultimately what canvassing, as well as organizing, is all about. "We raise money through the canvass, and we talk about issues," he said. "But when we train a canvasser, what we're really doing is training them how to move people, how to capture their imaginations, how to get them to make a commitment to something they care about." The point of the canvass, for him, is building the foundations for a long term, broad movement. "I tell people when they begin, 'You can trust me to work with you on a complementary basis. There's a career here, if you want. A minimal part is financial. But if you're the special kind of person who can do this for the long haul, there is a lot of reward.'"[9]

There are variations in canvass approaches and their affiliation with local organizing projects. Pam Bemis helped design a state canvass operation in Massachusetts, for Massachusetts Fair Share. State canvasses like Bemis's have recently joined in a national network with Citizen Action, called the Cooperative Alliance.[10]

Barbara Helmick, director of the national canvass of the Citizen Labor Energy Coalition, is one of the pioneers of the technique. She grew up in the farming community of Columbus Junction, Iowa, and has gone on to become a highly successful professional. Helmick had gone to a small private college, Monmouth, in downstate Illinois, but a semester at an urban Associated Colleges of the Midwest (ACM) studies program in Chicago in 1971 transformed her life. "The staff of the program just blasted us with analysis of social injustice," she remembers. "I went to my first women's consciousness raising group, and they were all talking about feminism. There must have been at least half of us sitting there, wondering what that was. I went home, looked it up in the dictionary, and thought, 'Well, that's what I am! I'm so glad there is a word for this.'"[11]

In the fall of 1973, Helmick saw an ad in the newspaper asking for people to interview for a position as "activist." "I thought, 'I'm an activist.'" So she applied.

The canvass had first been tried in 1971 by Marc Anderson, founder of the environmental organization called Citizens for a Better Environment in Chicago. CBE was closely connected to the community organizing scene in Chicago; indeed, when Helmick applied for the job, Anderson was attending a training session at the Midwest Academy. Anderson is the "father of social action canvassing." He insisted skillful business techniques could be combined with social commitment. It was a technique still in the process of development. Helmick, coming from a rural area, loved it. "Canvassing seemed the most obvious thing you should do, go to your neighbors and say, 'There's this problem. We all should do something.' I would go to a home with the complete expectation that most of them were going to agree with me." The canvass also seemed a chance to engage in political work that Helmick had assumed was missing from the 1970s. "I'd felt that I discovered the student movement too late. But here, political activity was still going on."

Anderson, creating a canvass network called Hudson Bay, worked with the Midwest Academy to develop ideas for how the new fundraising method might be combined with the new sorts of grass roots organizing. "I saw this as adding a new dimension to social change," he explained. "The canvass allowed us to reach ordinary citizens who had never before been touched by organizing." He and Helmick started travelling around to groups like Massachusetts Fair Share. "It fit the needs people saw, exactly," said Helmick. "Many of the groups were making the transition from city-wide to state-wide organization. They needed money. They needed ways to reach hundreds of thousands of people on issues. And they needed more people power." [12]

"Canvassing and organizing are different sorts of activities, but they can complement each other," says Anderson. The canvass does not itself create organizations. But it turned out to do far more than raise money. Chris Williams, a one-time environmental planner, had become convinced of the need for independent citizen organizing. He began canvassing for Indiana Citizen Action Coalition, formed by Fritz Wiecking and others to counter the power of special interests. Williams saw the canvass as an alternative source of information for the public. "The press simply hadn't covered the corruption that was going on around issues like utilities," explained Williams. "With the canvass, we were able to let people in key legislative districts know that the public service commission was controlled by the utility companies themselves. That led to a stampede for utility reform in the state legislature."

The canvass can educate large numbers of citizens about issues (even complex questions, like little-known aspects of utility regulation), identify people who are interested in becoming more active (both Doreen Del Bianco and Lynn Cardiff, for instance, made first contact with citizen groups through canvassers who came to their doors). And it generates specific sorts of support, like letters and signatures on petitions. In Massachusetts, for instance, the organization has set up a Citizens Lobby largely through the canvass operation. "It brings citizens directly into the organizing process itself," describes Pam Bemis. "With the Citizens

Lobby we identify people willing to write letters, contact their neighbors, get people to meetings, and serve as legislative coordinators."

Similarly, Citizen Action of New York has created a citizen action lobby line that is built on citizens who express an interest in being actively involved. "We see this as a way of broadening the constituencies interested in citizen action," explained canvass director Naya Pyskacek. "Most progressive information about issues is geared to other progressives, but the canvass is a way to talk directly to people who otherwise wouldn't get it." In Binghamton, New York, Citizen Action is employing its canvass in a human justice campaign around issues like comparable worth, ensuring that women and men who have similar training and job responsibilities receive comparable wages.[13]

Finally, it trains and educates many thousands of canvassers themselves for future political work. "You see increasing numbers of former canvassers in other parts of the Citizen Action network, and in other political work as well," observes Peter Rawson, canvass director for Connecticut Citizen Action Group. Rawson had continued canvassing after taking the job in 1981, partly because he enjoyed the hours and the atmosphere at work. But it also seemed to him different from a lot of other political activity. "We were involving people in CCAG and in the canvass from all sorts of backgrounds," he remembers. "And we were actually making change that was important to people, not just talking about it." The canvass turned out to be a training ground of its own. "The kinds of skills you learn through the canvass or being canvass director are very important for a career as an activist: how to communicate with many different kinds of people, how to supervise, how to listen, and knowledge about politics and organizing." For example, Mark Henry, who began as a canvasser for OPIC, now is on the Dayton City Council;[14] Betsy Reid, who was a canvasser for CLEC, is now political director for the American Federation of Government Employees; Kate Payton, once a canvass coordinator, is development director for the Peace Museum in Chicago.

Canvassing carries an alternative message that fits well with the public presence that citizen organizations were trying to convey. "The culture promotes a 'look out for number one' viewpoint that most people don't really agree with," argues Helmick. "But they don't see much alternative to it." What the canvass does, in her view, is emphasize people's connections to a broader community: "It reinforces the idea that we have a lot in common with our neighbors, and with the whole 'neighborhood' of people who are suffering economically and in other ways."[15]

In a similar vein, Larry Marx, a canvasser supervisor, observes that for many people, the canvass is their only yearly personal contact with a broader "public" that emphasizes a communal message. "Everybody's eyes always glance to their neighbors' signatures. A lot of times I get the reaction, 'I thought I was all alone on this problem.' The canvass validates people's feelings that the rules of the game are rigged, perceptions that on their own, alone, make them feel psychologically paranoid or off balance." For those who contribute or sign a petition or write a letter, the canvass can begin a concrete process that leads to further action. "It's a specific commitment," says Liz Blackburn, assistant director of the CLEC canvass. "People build on that. Next time they read an article in the paper about toxic wastes, they are less likely to think, 'That's a horrible problem that I can't do anything about,' and more, 'How can we beat the big companies that are doing that?'"[16]

Canvassing, of course, can vary widely in quality and sense of responsibility and impact on the organization itself. Canvassing is most effective when it is part of responsible, ongoing organizations that use it in concert with other organizing methods. As Sophie Ann Aoki, who works with the environmental organization Clean Water Action Project, puts it, "For organizations which use canvasses but have small or inactive memberships, for instance, it can become the tail that wags the dog."[17] Sophie Ann is skillful in the painstaking work of training canvassers, ensuring that they understand the organizational framework.

Experiences with the canvass do suggest, however, that irresponsible operations do not last very long. Canvasser turnover is high if the method is used simply as a fundraiser, without conveying a broader message of empowerment; and the public is soon turned off by overblown rhetoric, or failure to follow up with contacts and concrete results. Interestingly enough, the non-profit canvass works most effectively for broadly based, democratic populist organizations of the sort connected to Citizen Action, groups that champion a "public interest." For some years, canvass organizers anticipated counter efforts by the extreme right wing. "I thought we had only a year or two lead time over the right wing," says Marx. "When such efforts came, they flopped." When the oil and gas companies spent several million dollars in an attempt to get public support in favor of decontrol of natural gas prices, it proved a dismal failure. "Frankly, people saw through it," concludes Marx. "But the problem with the right generally is they have a hard time placing themselves in the shoes of the people they're talking to. They use the canvass instead to reinforce messages of division and powerlessness. A key to successful canvassing is being able to realize that we are part of the people we're communicating with." People who have been canvassed make the same point often. "I had never known there was such a group as Washington Fair Share, fighting for working people," explained one elderly woman who gave money for a utility rate campaign. "But these are people like me. We need something like this. I like it." [18]

In the early and mid-seventies, the very idea of getting a liveable salary for political work was sometimes controversial, among many veterans of sixties protests who had seen "organizing" and "movement work" as moral commitments alone. Community and citizen groups tended to be housed in out-of-the-way corners, church basements and the like, that were filled with rickety furniture, and they displayed casualness—often disinterest—about "conventional" practices like bookkeeping and accounting. Canvassing introduced a different sort of culture. "Operating a canvass program is not unlike running a small business," says Helmick. "Supervising staff, designing career development plans, keeping account of money, budgeting. This is a serious and business-like approach to social change. And it provided an important catalyst to many organizers in their transition from sixties styles of work to the seventies." [19]

Canvassing also helped broaden many organizers' perspectives on fundraising. "To some, it was not obvious that fundraising is political, especially in the early days," Helmick noted. "I think fundraising is the most critical part of the canvass. Not just because the money is needed. It's what it represents. While we inform folks out there on the issues, the most important piece of 'information' we give is that together we have the power to do something about these issues. Power comes from action.

It's not theoretical—we don't just inform people of this. We immediately reinforce the message—'Now that you realize acting brings change, act now, contribute.' The money we raise represents a commitment to action, and that is politically very significant."[20]

Because canvassing is so effective, politicians are constantly trying to prohibit it. In recent years there has been a growing tendency for towns and cities to find a legal pretext to keep canvassers out. Usually this takes the form of an ordinance prohibiting canvassing in the evening hours, the only time that working people are home. One reason commonly offered is that senior citizens need to be protected from solicitors or criminals at the door.

"Canvassing is protected by the First Amendment, as freedom of speech," says Tom Asher, the lawyer who has engaged in many of these legal battles.[21] The canvass as a means of communication affects many organizational decisions.

Larger citizen groups have often used the canvass as a way of testing the potential appeal of issues they are thinking about working on, or have first heard of issues from the responses of people door to door. "In Maryland," recounts Sue Jashinsky, canvass director in that state for several years, "people were telling us for some time that they wanted us to go after Baltimore Gas and Electric, the utility. We took it to the organizers and that became the main issue." In suburban communities like Friendly Hills, outside of Denver, Colorado, canvassers heard from families about the high incidence of cancer and other diseases among residents. A concerted investigation by the Colorado Citizens Action Network turned up a number of toxic waste sites. More broadly, the canvass on such a vast scale provided the growing Citizen Action organizations with a detailed and subtle feel for general public opinion that is largely lacking in other forms of activism and much politics. "Ronald Reagan's appeal is a mystery to most progressives," explained Mike Podhorzer, campaign director for national Citizen Action efforts. "But they are not talking to the 60 percent of Americans who voted for him. Sixty percent of the people our canvassers talk to every night voted for Reagan. What that does is enable an organization to be much more sensitive to the needs of the community."[22]

At the same time it provided a mechanism for getting a feel for general public concerns; moreover, the canvass taught a responsiveness to the particular languages of different communities. Marx, who had grown up in the Midwest, remembers the first time he tried canvassing in New York. "I was supposed to be this hotshot kid from Illinois. But in rural Illinois, everybody says, 'Hi, how are you?' They talk about the weather, and slowly warm up to the subject. On Staten Island, in five seconds it was 'What's the bottom line, son?' I thought first I couldn't do it at all." Sue Jashinsky found it important to regularly offer training sessions on particular neighborhoods. "The canvassers have to learn to be good listeners, to figure out what the neighborhood is like and what will motivate people. So we do whole briefings on a neighborhood. What do they care about? What do they buy? You go through a whole community profile, before you even talk about the issues." Ethnic communities, for instance, think in terms of the neighborhood, the parish, the family, threats to such community institutions, and the need for neighbors to pull together. "When you're canvassing," as Vicki Sipe, canvass director of Iowa Citizen Action Network, puts it, "you're building coalitions. So, like other coalitions, you work from the experience and self-interest of the group you are talking to. You deal with people on their own terms." [23]

David Zwick, another pioneer of the method, who directs Clean Water Action Project, describes it as "a mass communications method, much more personal and connected than other techniques. You have ways to reach large numbers of people beyond your block or group or town. It creates a gigantic educational process, a kind of infrastructure for a democratic movement." Zwick came to the canvass after serving in Vietnam during the war, and searching for a way to constructively express social concerns. He has established canvasses for many environmental groups including the League of Conservation Voters.

The canvass message is constantly shaped and transformed by the interaction between citizen organization and public. The canvass is an ongoing, if abbreviated, dialogue, about public life that in many ways people are hungry for. "I remember people who would give me money who say they disagree with us about the issues, but they're glad we're out here stirring up debate," Diane Jensen, a canvasser in Minnesota and Illinois, recalls.

The canvass in some ways is an encounter characteristic of public life in modern society. It is brief and highly structured, for instance. But it also points beyond, toward a richer, more community-grounded sense of participation and democracy.[24] Most important, perhaps, it should be seen as a developing medium for a movement that is still in its early stages. It provided a base for the national network of organizations, Citizen Action, and continues to tie together Citizen Action and many other progressive groups—environmentalists, the peace activists, and others—that also use a canvass.

Canvass directors like to ground the work in the broader vision and tradition of those who have struggled over time for a more democratic society. "If you don't focus on the daily margin of difference you make, you're not going to be in it for the long term," explains Larry Marx. Informational briefings for staff emphasize such a movement tradition. "I describe everything from the National Farmers Alliances of the first Populists to the Committees of Correspondence in the American Revolution," Marx continues. "Alliance organizers would go door to door collecting two dollars a year from dirt poor farmers and selling the *Appeal to Reason*, the radical newspaper in the Southwest. It had what they called the 'Soldier Salesperson Army,' organized with captains and sergeants, using everything from foot to bicycles to buggies to get out the word." [25]

In this vein, canvass leaders see their work as keeping alive a democratic vision through hard times and preparing the ground for the future. "I believe the canvass, and all the thousands of people who have come through it, is one important reason why progressive ideas are still alive," says Jashinsky. Like that of many other young people in the seventies and eighties, Jashinsky's discovery of the opportunities to "get paid to do political work" came as a kind of godsend, after believing that activism had died out. She now spends a considerable time recruiting high school students.[26]

Periodically, canvassers have experiences that seem a foretaste of the sort of generalized spirit and energy characteristic of broad social movements. "When I go into a working class community like East Boston or

Roxbury or Dorchester," describes Jessica Hallowell, now canvass director in Boston, Massachusetts, "I don't get much money from any particular house. But every home gives money, even if it's not a lot. People know we're working directly with them and for them. It's the people's organization, and what we do affects them directly." Vicki Sipe remembers canvassing on a hot Saturday afternoon in the small working class town of Crystal, Minnesota. The neighborhood was slab concrete, poorer homes. But people responded enthusiastically to both the issues and the idea of getting together to fight for control over their lives. "There was not a single person that entire afternoon who said 'No' or 'You're wrong' or 'There's nothing we can do about it,'" Sipe remembers. "Everybody gave me two or three dollars, took me from house to house, introduced me to their neighbors. After a while I didn't even have to knock on the door. I came out with my quota, but also with more warmth and coffee and cake and pie and happiness than I'd ever had." To Helmick, "Canvassers gain energy from our supporters" and simultaneously "carry the spirit of that belief with them from home to home, connecting and igniting the spirit."[27]

In many ways, the canvass is also still a relatively new and unexplored tool of organizing and communications—and one about which almost nothing has been written. Despite the numbers it reaches, those who pioneered and now direct the national operations still see it now fulfilling only a small part of its potential for outreach.

But it is also a tool that has proved its power in national campaigns that have required contacting and mobilizing very large numbers of Americans. No campaign has been more challenging than the one waged for four years against the combined might of America's largest complex of corporations, the empire of Big Oil and its political allies.

As farm auctions increased, so too did the cry, "No sale! No sale!" Citizen action organizers worked alongside farmers to stop foreclosures.

Citizen groups fight for energy at a price people can afford. Here the Ohio Public Interest Campaign protests Construction Work in Progress (CWIP), a device that allows utilities to charge customers for uncompleted power plants. (Photo: John Colm)

Many groups rallied behind the effort to stop natural gas price hikes. In 1982 and 1983, citizen action groups organized farmers and others in this effort. (Photo: Lenora Davis)

The break-up of AT&T gave rise to new citizen campaigns to guarantee affordable telephone service. Here members of Oregon Fair Share protest a hike in telephone access charges.

Senior citizens are a critical part of the coalitions. Seniors are a leading force in the Florida Consumer Federation, where they won victories to stop health insurance and telephone rate hikes.

In 1984, Miles Rapoport, former director of Connecticut Citizen Action Group, was elected to the state legislature. His campaign was a model of grass roots organizing that relied on heavy voter contact and volunteer recruitment.

Citizen Action groups gather annually at their state capitols to press for progressive legislation. In 1983, Citizen Action Coalition of Indiana held a state lobby day to promote populist employment and energy policy. In the same year, Wisconsin Action Coalition brought seven hundred unionists and community and senior activists to their capitol.

Professional door-to-door canvassers play a major role in building the new citizen movement. Along with the money they raise, these canvassers generate grass roots support for progressive programs. (Photo: Lenora Davis)

Americans are increasingly alarmed by the rising threat of hazardous waste.
(Photo: George Terrell)

Connecticut Citizen Action Group pioneered innovative approaches to clean up hazardous waste. Today hundreds of citizen groups are involved in efforts to clean up toxic substances.

The Midwest Academy annual retreat has become an exciting national gathering for discussing the direction of the new populism. (Photo: Marc Pokempner)

Long time southern activist Cora Tucker tells those at the Midwest Academy retreat her vision for a better America. (Photo: Kennedy Wheatley)

Members of the Citizen Labor Energy Coalition and Illinois Public Action Council celebrate their victories at the 1984 Labor Day parade in Chicago. (Photo: Syd Harris)

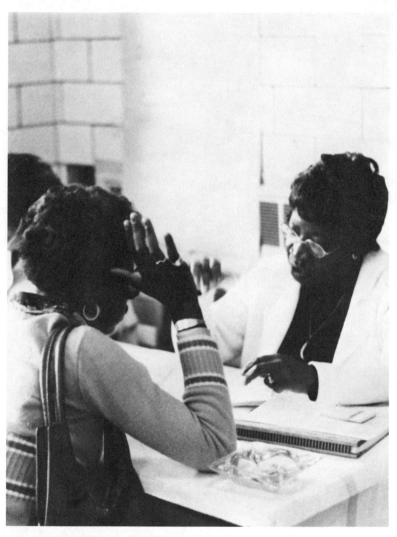

Across the nation voter registration has become a key tool for people's empowerment.

"Our goal is to put the people first." Pictured at a Citizen Labor Energy Coalition board meeting are Robert Brandon, director of CLEC; William Winpisinger, president of the International Association of Machinists; Heather Booth, co-director of Citizen Action; and Bill Hutton, executive director of the National Council of Senior Citizens. (Photo: Bill Burke)

"People like you help people like me go on," sings songwriter and organizer Si Kahn, with Jan Schakowsky, from Illinois, and Karen Thomas, past director of the Midwest Academy. (Photo: Kenneth Wheatley)

Hundreds marched in Richmond, Virginia, protesting Reagan budget cuts. Similar coalitions sprang up across the U.S. (Photo: Gary Burns, Richmond Times-Dispatch*)*

5. ENERGY POLITICS

We Beat Big Oil.

Canvasser button

The long line of black limousines outside the John Hancock tower in downtown Chicago gave the impression that some diplomatic crisis might be occurring. But in the exclusive restaurant high atop the building, chief executives of Exxon were simply holding a party. The occasion was the annual convention of the American Petroleum Institute, the oil industry's lobbying arm. Spirits ran high that night, November 8, 1981, just one year after the sweeping Republican victory. With enthusiastic backing from the new president and clear indications that majorities in both House and Senate supported them as well, oil executives confidently looked forward to swift enactment of their main legislative priority—a lifting of remaining price controls from natural gas.

Suddenly, the elevators opened. A large crowd of men and women of all ages, appearance, and dress poured out, talking, singing songs, laughing. "You can't come in here," yelled one executive in elegant attire. "We're Exxon International!" The group of protesters paid no attention. They asked to have a meeting with Exxon chairman Clifton Garvin. In response, the executives hid, hoping the crowd would soon disappear. But the next day, the scene was more alarming yet. From thirty states, by train, bus, car, on foot, and on Chicago's elevated train, five thousand angry citizens converged on the API convention site. In the chill fall air, they cheered, carried signs, and chanted so loudly the executives meeting inside could hear all too well: "Stop big oil!"; "Stop natural gas decontrol!"; "Freeze prices, not senior citizens!" remembered William Hutton, director of the National Council of Senior Citizens and secretary-treasurer of the Citizen Labor Energy Coalition, which co-sponsored the demonstration with National People's Action, an alliance of neighborhood groups across the country. "It was inspiring," he said. "Young and old, black and white, unionists and farmers and housewives came together to tell the oil companies our lives and futures are at stake. We're ready to fight."[1]

The event signalled the beginning of a visible, national, and massive campaign. It was to result in one of the administration's biggest setbacks in its first term. "We're developing into something more than a consumer movement," Robert Creamer, director of Illinois Public Action, told the *Los Angeles Times*. "This is the surfacing of the people in political action," Creamer elaborated. "This is the beginning of a movement to reclaim our country for those who built it and make it run." The populist organizing that had spread over a decade was making its first sustained and large scale appearance on the national scene.[2]

When the Citizen Labor Energy Coalition formed in the spring of 1978, it built upon several years of scattered, local protests against the energy companies that had begun in the wake of the Oil Embargo of 1973. Despite public outcry at price increases and shortages, which many experts believed were largely contrived, the energy giants continued to consolidate strength. Indeed, their influence reached into every crevice of the political system. When Jimmy Carter declared the energy crisis "the moral equivalent of war" and sought to enact a comprehensive energy policy in 1977, the nine members of the Senate Finance Committee passed a lavish series of subsidies and tax breaks for oil and gas companies. The senators also were recipients of more than $547,000 in contributions from the industry. Nowhere was the power of Big Oil more vivid than on the question of gas price decontrol.[3]

By the 1970s, the large oil companies controlled more than 50 percent of natural gas supplies. Six of the eight largest gas producers were among the eight largest oil producers, accounting for more than 40 percent of gas sales. Through coordinating and political groups like the Natural Gas Supply Committee and the American Petroleum Institute, the oil and gas companies developed strategy and political clout.[4]

The energy empire moved into action with vigor during the energy battles of 1977. For years, energy industry spokespersons had argued that controls on natural gas prices, first enacted in 1938, reduced the incentives to look for new gas supplies and thus threatened the country. In 1968, however, the Supreme Court ruled that market regulation was fair, noting that, according to the industry's own records, more gas had been found every year than was burned by consumers.

In the aftermath of the court decision, industry figures of available reserves began showing a sharp decline and company executives through the 1970s warned each year of looming shortages. In response—although James Halverson, director of the Federal Trade Commission's Bureau of Competition, warned that gas reserves were being underreported by as much as 1,000 percent in some areas—the Federal Power Commission under President Ford rapidly increased the prices of natural gas between 1972 and 1976, allowing new gas sold in interstate commerce to rise by more than 300 percent.[5]

Figures from the government were almost wholly derived from those the industry gave it. In the midst of the 1977 debates, Senator John Durkin said the information available left him totally in the dark about whether "we are running out of natural gas or swimming in it. . . . We sit here today like map makers of centuries ago, attempting to chart unseen lands by relying on secondhand information."[6]

At the grass roots, ordinary citizens knew little about such deliberations. But they did know they found it increasingly impossible to pay their energy bills. In northern cities like Philadelphia, senior citizens found themselves without heat in the midst of winter. "My feet froze up in January," described one elderly woman on the west side, "but I didn't have enough money to put the heat back on." In Kansas, farmers worried that mounting energy costs would add to the already grave threats facing their farms. "I don't know if we can pay," explained one farmer whose land had been in the family for nearly a century. "If the heating bills for the cows go up much more, we may lose this place."[7]

At first, Carter officials seemed to respond to such concerns. They showed considerable skepticism about corporate claims and challenged corporate arguments and pointed out that decontrol would tie U.S. energy prices even more closely to the policies of the OPEC cartel. They maintained that gas price decontrol would cost consumers $70 billion by 1985 and predicted that "the vast majority" of an estimated thirty to forty-five years' worth of recoverable gas supplies left in the country could be produced for costs that would return ample profit. Yet industry pressure was intense. When two congressmen introduced an industry bill for immediate decontrol, House Speaker Tip O'Neill commented that "never have I seen such an influx of lobbyists in this town." Moreover, the influence of pro-oil industry advisers like Robert Strauss was steadily growing. And Carter, according to Senator Howard Metzenbaum, was desperate to get "any sort of bill at all." The result was an abrupt change in the administration position. It endorsed a gradual decontrol of prices on new gas (which is gas that was discovered after 1977) with a complete lifting of controls on such gas by 1985. After a bitter battle, the measure passed. And as a result, gas prices began climbing rapidly, at a rate more than three times that of inflation.[8]

The new Citizen Labor Energy Coalition was not in a position to fight back effectively against the 1977 partial decontrol of prices. But it anticipated the importance of gas prices and other energy issues in the coming years in shaping the broader character of politics. In the initial policy statement proposed for CLEC, William Winpisinger and Heather Booth (CLEC's first president and director respectively) wrote that "energy policy must be regarded as an avenue to broader national goals."

Winpisinger, as president of the Machinists union had been enthusiastic about this sort of joint effort with consumers as essential to revitalizing the labor movement. He said, "This is more than a matter of dollars and cents. This is a question of who owns America. What our country stands for. Where we are going." Booth believed that efforts around energy politics "would provide the chance to come together across the divisions which had torn apart so many groups in the 1960s. This is a chance to rebuild a sense of who we are as *Americans*, as a whole people."[9]

CLEC's first national event, "Big Oil Day," October 17, 1979, brought out fifty thousand people in more than 120 cities across the country in support of a program that included:

Reimposition of controls on oil and natural gas
Establishment of a publicly owned energy corporation
Horizontal and vertical divestiture of the major oil companies
Elimination of the oil depletion allowance
Establishment of a solar development bank
Funding for low income energy assistance and weatherization
    programs.

Seven thousand citizens protested in the Federal Plaza in Chicago; one thousand seniors picketed the American Petroleum Institute offices in Washington; eight hundred people from community, labor, and other groups marched under the banner of CLEC in Charleston, West Virginia. They were joined by the Progressive Alliance, a coalition of groups headed by Doug Fraser, then president of the United Auto Workers union. In response, several oil companies announced rollbacks in prices of heating oil, and the governors of Connecticut and Minnesota called legislative sessions to provide emergency assistance for the forthcoming winter. In a longer term sense, the day marked the beginning of local organization that would lay foundations for future national campaigns.[10]

For the next two years, CLEC concentrated on campaigns with considerable local focus, around issues like bans on shutoff of utilities during the winter to those unable to pay, utility rate reform, and state taxes on oil profits that had been shifted from state to state to avoid taxation. Through such organizing, local foundations developed for concerted national efforts in the future.

"I grew up poor and I was told time and time again, 'You can't fight City Hall,'" remembered Bill Moore, vice president of New Hampshire People's Alliance, an affiliate of both CLEC and Citizen Action. But through the People's Alliance, Moore had learned a different lesson. The group began state-wide organizing in May, 1979. On May 1 of that year, culminating a twenty-one month campaign of demonstrations, testimony at hearings, and other tactics, the organization won a major victory when the public utilities commission agreed with the group's proposal for a universal lifeline electric rate structure. Under the plan, per-unit rates for the first two hundred kilowatt-hours of electricity are no higher than those per-unit rates charged to large businesses and institutions, which residences had previously subsidized. Residential customers' bills fell by more than 20 percent. But the experience of victory for members of the People's Alliance was equally important. "It also makes clear that low and moderate-income people can build and exercise real power by taking action together," explained Larry Converse of Claremont, president of the group. CLEC groups in Washington, Idaho, Maryland, Oregon, and a number of other states made reform of utility rate structures major campaigns.[11]

The experience in CLEC helped to mobilize people in coalition on other issues. In Wisconsin, the Wisconsin Action Coalition was born out of CLEC. "Even more important than the reforms is the fact that all segments of organized labor, neighborhood groups, and senior citizen organizations worked together," said Dan Kaemmerer of Wisconsin Action Coalition. As a result, the group looked forward to "a new era of political activism in Wisconsin" that could propose and win constructive solutions for a state economy wracked by plant shutdowns, farm foreclosures, and a mounting state debt. "CLEC was the beginning," said Earl Lepp, secretary treasurer of the Milwaukee County Labor Council, who became a leader in the new group. "Since then, we've begun to get some real political clout for the coalition."[12]

When he was going to college at the University of Maryland in the 1960s, Kenneth Montague faced frequent problems as one of the first blacks to enter that institution. One time an English professor accused him of plagiarizing an essay on Edmund Spencer because she doubted that a black could actually write such a penetrating piece of work. Montague was furious. "My philosophy is that what I get, I earn. I would never plagiarize anything in my life." He had a sense of heritage and roots, gained from a childhood on a farm, that strengthened him. "I would say, 'What's the bottom line?' I don't have to do all the things people tell me I have to do because I can always go back to the land, which will produce simply if I work. That gave me confidence." His roots and subsequent experiences in the Peace Corps in Africa, through which he learned "the power of individual effort," proved him in good stead when he settled into the northeastern section of Baltimore as a young lawyer in the 1970s.[13]

Montague took a leading role in stabilizing the process of integration. "The real estate companies were trying to panic all the whites into leaving so they could buy their houses cheaply and sell them at high prices to blacks." The community organization in the community, North East Community Organization, or NECO, had taken a position in favor of integration, but against the fear tactics of the real estate interests, and Montague had chaired its conservation zone committee, which designed the strategy. It led to work on city-wide issues. "I had seen the value of organizing," he described. "The fact was that people felt tolerance as individuals if they came together and expressed their concerns, and that when a multitude got together, they began to be a political force. So then I started to dream. We could do that for the whole city."

Montague had also chaired the NECO energy commission, working on issues especially of concern to low income people in the community. When he heard about CLEC, a new coalition forming in Baltimore to work on energy issues, he talked to the organizer, Ann Feldman. "What she said really made sense. They were talking not only about Baltimore but the whole state."

Montague described himself as "a mild-mannered person unless I get angry." At a crucial meeting not long after CLEC had formed in the state, his anger proved a watershed for the group. The Baltimore utility, Baltimore Gas and Electric, or BG&E, was shutting off the utilities of people who could not keep up with their bills, even in the coldest part of the winter. Against the background of unemployment reaching 20 percent in the early 1980s, that meant not only the poor. "We went to the utility and said, 'These are people who would normally pay their bills. They've successfully participated. You've got to give people credit.'" But the company was intransigent. Then CLEC asked for a meeting with the chairman of the BG&E board, Bernard Treushler. Montague headed the delegation.

They met in the board chief's office, fifteen members of CLEC on one side of a long, elegant wooden table, the executive and his top aides on the other. Around the walls hung expensive paintings; the floors were richly carpeted with Oriental rugs. Many of the poor people in the delegation were nervous.

"We had asked for the meeting and had an agenda," Montague remembered. "But the head of the BG and E board said he should chair the meeting. He didn't seem to get the message. He and I had words—I was trying to proceed and let him know the ground rules." They both raised up in their chairs. Treushler said, "Who gave you permission to chair this meeting?"

Montague's entire history came back to him—the confidence he had learned from the land, from his time in the Peace Corps, from his organizing experience. "It was a question of someone looking at me as a black man and figuring I had to have permission. It made me angry." Other people describing the scene say that at one point Montague told Treushler that he could leave—his own office—if he didn't like it. Montague recalled simply saying, "Who the hell are you to give me permission to do anything?" The meeting proceeded. CLEC won its demand for an end to shutoffs. And as in Wisconsin, Oregon, Idaho, Iowa, and other states, the coalition decided to become a multi-issue citizen organization, called Maryland Citizen Action Coalition.

By 1983, CLEC had affiliates coast to coast:

Citizens Action League in California
California CLEC
Colorado CLEC
Iowa CLEC
Maryland CLEC
Missouri CLEC
New York CLEC
Connecticut Citizen Action Group
Florida Consumer Federation
Illinois Public Action Council
Citizens Action Coalition of Indiana

Massachusetts Fair Share
Minnesota COACT
New Hampshire People's Alliance
New Jersey Citizen Action
Ohio Public Interest Campaign
Oregon Fair Share
Pennsylvania Public Interest Coalition
Rhode Island Community Labor Coalition
Virginia Action
West Virginia Citizen Action Group
Wisconsin Action Coalition.

In addition, CLEC had parallel organizing efforts in other states, including Kentucky, Michigan, Kansas, Idaho, and Washington—the last two groups soon to become Fair Share organizations. The CLEC canvass, directed by Barbara Helmick, had been initiated just before Big Oil Day in 1979. By the beginning of 1983, the canvass network had offices in Washington, D.C.; Philadelphia; Baltimore; Milwaukee; Minneapolis; Pittsburgh; Hackensack and New Brunswick, New Jersey; Harrisburg, Pennsylvania; Waterloo and Iowa City, Iowa; Denver, Colorado; and several other cities. With such a base, it was able to sustain a serious campaign against the very center of the American power structure itself, the empire of Big Oil.[14]

By 1981, the evidence about the "need for incentives" to produce more gas seemed specious, indeed. "The gas potential of the U.S. is almost beyond comprehension," said Michael Halbouty of Houston, a leading expert on energy and head of the Reagan energy policy task force during the election campaign. "It is completely safe to say we have enough gas to take us well into the twenty-first century." Growth in production had been so swift that many areas of the country had excesses of gas, with reservoirs filled to capacity.[15]

Yet oil industry supporters were nonetheless confident they could decontrol all prices of gas and crafted a two-part strategy to accomplish the goal. First, the administration planned to introduce legislation along the lines of plans worked out by a special group, headed by James Watt and David Stockman. The legislation would immediately decontrol the price of all "new" gas and speed the price increases for "old" gas to reach the equivalent prices of OPEC oil by 1985. Second, the administration planned to use a little-known but powerful agency, called the Federal Energy Regulatory Commission, or FERC, as a means to speed the process further by shifting gas from "old" and more regulated categories into "hard-to-find" categories already decontrolled—whose price was twice as high. With the power to appoint three of the five seats on FERC, including the chair, the administration seemed to have assured control of the regulatory agency. Moreover, its apparent insensitivity to the human costs of decontrol seemed without limit. When elderly persons and health officials protested that heating costs were preventing many senior citizens from heating their homes, leading to alarming increases in hypothermia, they saw a government brochure that recommended that seniors should "wrap newspapers around their feet." CLEC responded. In February, the coalition affiliates and projects in forty-three states declared their intention to stop complete decontrol.[16]

In 1981, CLEC was directed by Robert Brandon, a lawyer who had previously directed Ralph Nader's Tax Research Group. He was able to combine the skills of lobbying and analysis with sensitivity to the timing of grass roots campaigns. "Our goal was to move the debate out of Washington, D.C., and into the homes, small businesses, and factories that were going to suffer damage from these policies," Brandon said. Debating complex energy policies in the marble halls of Congress under the influence of the oil and gas companies would continue industry domination of gas policies. "We assisted people by supplying the facts, exposing consumer friends and foes, and mobilizing for grass roots pressure. We were able to turn friends into advocates and forced many foes to retreat by highlighting the real majority will in their districts."[17] The Citizen Labor Energy Coalition was able to draw on groups working in the area of energy policy for a variety of crucial resources. None was more pivotal than research.

Soon after the oil embargo in 1973, a group of progressive and populist citizen advocates, including Miles Rubin, economist Stanley Sheinbaum, and such notables as Paul Newman, founded Energy Action as a research and action group. "We thought it was critical that the American people be able to get the facts about energy and then gain some say in the energy policy debates," explained Rubin. It quickly became a much used source of accurate, in-depth information. When CLEC was established, Energy Action's director, Jim Flug and his assistant Barbara Shailor, brought the organization in. It continued to provide crucial research capabilities. In 1981, Ed Rothschild, then director of Energy Action, released a study on a state-by-state basis that showed the real cost of energy production. The study was to prove a crucial part of the battle.[18]

From the beginning the coalition developed a three-part strategy as counter to the industry. "The first principle," read a CLEC document analyzing the coalition's effort, "was to set the debate on consumers' terms—educating the media, the public, and the Congress on the impact of decontrol before the oil companies could begin their own propaganda campaign. The second principle was to wage an offensive campaign, seeking pledges from members of Congress to vote against decontrol. And the third principle, perhaps the most important, was to integrate the grass roots capabilities of community organizations, labor, and seniors into a combined force that could hold members of Congress accountable for their positions."[19]

By March 7, 1982, when President Reagan officially asked Congress to implement decontrol, strong campaigns had already been begun by OPIC, Citizen Action Coalition, or CAC, in Indiana, and Illinois Public Action Council. In June, the AFL-CIO formally joined in the effort and together with CLEC released *Pipeline to Disaster*, another study on the impact of decontrol that predicted 3.4 million jobs would be lost by 1985 if all controls were lifted. The campaign identified in particular twenty-five priority Democrats and Republicans who could swing large numbers of votes. With accountability sessions in districts across the country, the coalition sought to get them to declare publicly their opposition to administration plans.[20]

The local dimension made an immense difference. "Up until that point," explained Mike Podhorzer, campaign director, "people would use national facts like it will cost a hundred billion dollars. But we figured out how to translate that into the local level in specific states. How much of tax cuts would be erased by gas decontrol, that kind of thing." The approach, by definition in a far flung confederation of groups like CLEC, involved considerable discussion. "We would never impose things, but look for ways that what was happening nationally could be helpful locally." Don Wiener and Brad Karkkainen co-ordinated the field organizing. They developed common tactics that could be adapted to the specifics of particular areas. In Indiana, CAC got small businesses to take out ads in the newspaper, asking their conservative Republican congressman why he was in favor of high gas bills. Pressure in Ohio forced Republican Governor James Rhodes to oppose decontrol on the grounds it "would help destroy homeowners, drive industry from Ohio and destroy countless jobs." The Midwest Governors' Association, with many Republican members, took a position against decontrol in October. Altogether, coalition affiliates organized two hundred meetings in congressional districts. And they mixed such a tactic with demonstrations across the country. The canvass proved a critical tool in the campaign.[21]

Sue Jashinsky was recruited to the canvass in Milwaukee by an ad that said, "Fight Big Oil." But when she started out in the southern areas of the city, she was doubtful. "I thought, 'Come on, people don't know anything about that issue.' But I was wrong. People were really interested. And year after year they became more sophisticated on natural gas." Similarly, Pat Englert, beginning to canvass in New Jersey, was surprised at the public interest. "It was real heartening. I remember an older woman who said, 'I don't have time to talk, I'm rushed.' I said I wanted to talk about her gas bill a minute. And she said, 'What!?' pulled me inside, and sat me down. She knew more about the issue than I did." Canvassers, conducting a massive public information campaign, contacted nearly two million households in the initial effort.[22]

Eighteen of the twenty-five key targeted congress people agreed to oppose decontrol plans publicly, and three others became convinced that they should lose interest in the issue. By March, 1982, President Reagan appeared to back down, announcing that he would not try to get decontrol legislation passed that year. It turned out to be simply a shift of strategy. "Wisely the industry decided to avoid a fight over principle and to take the back door to deregulation," reported *Forbes* magazine, describing a "private meeting" between Exxon chairman Clifton Garvin and presidential counselor Edwin Meese. As a result, the FERC made plans for "backdoor decontrol" by shifting gas from one category to another.[23]

But CLEC responded vigorously with a strategy that called for "politicizing FERC." CLEC leaders supported a resolution in Congress sponsored by John Dingell of Michigan that instructed the agency not to quicken the pace of decontrol. And the coalition demanded FERC hold field hearings in communities affected by higher prices. When FERC came to a field meeting in Columbus, Ohio, the Ohio Public Interest Campaign turned out seven hundred citizens to confront Representative Clarence "Bud" Brown, a leading supporter of gas decontrol who was testifying. By April, a majority of the House, 227 congressmen, had co-sponsored the Dingell resolution. Later that year, CLEC and Citizen Action targeted several key politicians who had supported decontrol. The Indiana Citizen Action Coalition and CLEC helped Frank McCloskey unseat incumbent Joel Deckard. In West Virginia, Bob Wise, former chairman of West Virginia CLEC, upset incumbent Mick Stanton in the Third District. In New York, Robert Mrazek beat right wing Congressman John Le Boutillier in a campaign during which CLEC canvassers knocked on thirty thousand doors to let his constituents know his consistent support of the oil companies. In Ohio, OPIC, revealing that the incumbent Republican congressman had received lavish oil and gas contributions, aided neighborhood leader Marcy Kaptur to win in her first try at public office. Of the thirty-five candidates whom CLEC endorsed for Congress, thirty were elected, including ten new members of the House.[24]

With such successes, CLEC moved to the offensive, putting together a package to "recontrol" the prices of gas, rolling them to 1982 levels, and putting permanent controls on old gas. In 1983, the administration and the coalition forces battled over contending pieces of legislation in the House and Senate. Industry strategists and the New Right fought back fiercely in favor of administration efforts to win decontrol. The Natural Gas Supply Association spent one million dollars to create a front, the Alliance for Energy Security, that sought to conduct large scale phone and canvass campaigns. Richard Viguerie tried a direct mail operation, seeking to mobilize support "against the bureaucrats in Washington" in order to support the oil companies. Both flopped miserably. The press picked up the story that the major oil and gas producers paid forty-five thousand dollars each for the canvass campaign. Mobil Oil took out full page ads in the *Washington Post* and *New York Times* entitled "Danger: Mythmaker at Work," responding to CLEC figures on the corporate profits.[25]

The final votes on November 16 showed the coalition still not strong enough to pass its wide ranging reforms. But the major oil companies' legislation and the administration had become isolated on the issue. Their decontrol legislation lost in the Senate by a vote of 67 to 28. The meaning of the campaign, moreover, was summarized best by industry groups themselves. "Big oil has less influence at the grassroots level," said one lobbyist for Phillips Petroleum. The Human Resources Network, which describes itself as a "planning service for management," concluded in a publication on the gas decontrol fight that the issue "has become a question of coalition building, lobbying, and grassroots political organizing." The work of the coalition had changed the very nature of the argument. According to the publication, the coalition had "been able to define decontrol as an issue of costs, rather than of market mechanisms versus government regulation." From the perspective of those who had led the fight for years, moreover, it was a vivid indication of what a concerted and unified effort could accomplish. "Nobody thought we could do it in the beginning," reflected William Winpisinger. He laughed. "But this has changed the nature of coalition building, raised our sense of what is powerful. The people are finally winning one."[26]

A retrospective look at the changes in energy politics suggests the importance of united grass roots activism and its translation into the national level, alike. Prior to the formation of CLEC, energy policy had been dominated almost exclusively by those concentrated corporate interests that were organized to pursue their own self-interests. Oil companies, gas and electric utilities, coal producers, and others understood the stakes. They were prepared to do battle at every level, from the grass roots to the nation's capital.

Opposition groups were small, underfinanced, mostly Washington-based, and often involved in an array of other issues besides energy. The

Citizen Labor Energy Coalition for the first time brought many of these groups together under one roof. It was able to identify issues of mutual concern and devise strategies for addressing these issues, organize new groups at local and state levels, and coordinate the efforts of thousands of citizens in pursuit of energy policies that protected consumers, workers, and communities.

CLEC's energy policy has evolved over the years into a broader vision for a more democratic, participatory, and responsive energy system.

Today, energy corporations restrict competition through either private arrangements or government intervention. CLEC is convinced that when the nation's anti-trust laws are violated, law and order must prevail. Without tough, swift, and unrelenting anti-trust enforcement, small businesses, consumers, and communities will fall prey to collusion, price fixing, and other illegal activities. The transportation and distribution of natural gas and electricity are conducted, for the most part, by utility monopolies. A democratic vision would develop alternatives to utility monopolies like municipally and publicly owned electric and gas companies. Such municipal and local ownership not only leaves decisions in the hands of the communities affected but also ensures that revenues generated remain in those communities. Such a vision holds that citizens, through our government and other means, must play a central role in other policy areas, including taxation, public lands, research and development, environmental protection, electric utility and natural gas pipeline regulation, and foreign policy.

The real costs of producing energy are often not reflected in its price. There are extraordinary societal costs that come from the excessive pollution and environmental degradation caused by the production of fossil and nonrenewable fuels. These costs are felt from polluted rivers and lakes, toxic waste dumps, stripmined land, and human suffering from environmental diseases like black lung and the cancers that are caused by workplace exposures to many petrochemicals. Thus, rapid expansion of renewable energy resources and conservation are critical to the development of a more healthy environment and an active ethos of stewardship over the earth's resources.

The U.S. government spends hundreds of millions of dollars a year on energy research and development. The bulk of this money is spent in the areas of nuclear power and fossil fuels, and comparatively little is spent on conservation and solar and other renewable energy sources. CLEC believes that these priorities must be shifted. The long term benefits of development and expansion of solar energy are well known—human scale technology, increased jobs, reduced pollution, and inexhaustible supply. As director of CLEC Bob Brandon commented, "Basic needs like heat and electricity should be a basic right that people can afford. Energy can be efficient and safe and not subject to monopoly control. The people must come first, and they must take the lead in designing and implementing energy policy." [27]

The politics of energy has raised questions of value, harm, loss to communities and regions, and the like in the rarified debates about economic policy. Such a process began to happen in other areas as well, sometimes dramatically. In the case of the fight against toxic waste dumping, the issues sometimes involved matters of life and death.

6. PLAGUES ON THE LAND

*Then God said, "And now we will make human beings; they will
be like us and resemble us; they will have power over the fish, the
birds, and all animals, domestic and wild, large and small." So God
created human beings, . . . male and female, blessed them, and said,
"Have many children, so that your descendents will live all over the
earth and bring it under their control. I am putting you in charge of
the fish, the birds, and all the wild animals."*

Genesis 1:26–27

*So they took ashes from the kiln, and stood before Pharoah, and
Moses threw them toward heaven, and it became boils breaking
out in sores on man and beast. And the magicians could not stand
before Moses because of the boils, for the boils were upon the
magicians and upon all the Egyptions.*

Exodus 9:10–11

Slowly, on a cold, windy night on December 6, 1984, white gas seeped
from the tanks of the Union Carbide plant and spread across the
shantytowns in Bhopal, India, where thousands of families slept. Swapan
Saha, a sociologist staying in a nearby hotel, woke suddenly. "It was both

a burning and a suffocating sensation," he remembered, "like breathing fire." Wrapping a towel around his face, Saha went outside. A huge crowd milled around in panic; many writhed on the ground, next to pigs and cattle. "The next morning," reported *Newsweek*, "it looked like a neutron bomb had struck. Buildings were undamaged. But humans and animals littered the low ground, turning hilly Bhopal into a city of corpses."[1]

News of the horrifying gas leak in Bhopal reached Institute, West Virginia, where a Union Carbide plant called Uncle John's produced methyl isocyanate, the same chemical that killed twenty-five hundred and injured up to a hundred thousand on the other side of the world. Company officials had heard warnings the previous September that the plant in Institute might experience a "runaway reaction" like that which occurred in Bhopal—and had taken no action. After the disaster, they issued reassurances that "it couldn't happen here."

But frightened local residents decided to take action themselves. "We had to do something—we knew we could no longer trust the company," explained one long time resident. "Our homes and families were at stake."[2]

They called a town meeting to talk about what to do. Responding to community alarm, Union Carbide temporarily closed its plant. Soon, the company announced plans for a five-million-dollar program to improve safety and warning systems. The plan was a victory for community activists and for West Virginia Citizen Action Group, a citizen organization that had fought for several years to ensure stricter safety standards on chemical companies. But it was far from solving the problem. The following August, a chemical storage tank at the plant leaked toxic gas across the town. One hundred thirty-four people were treated for breathing problems, burning eyes, nausea, and dizziness. The warning siren had not sounded any alarm until nearly a half hour after the crisis. In nearby Charleston, meanwhile, medical researchers found rates of cancer far higher than those in the rest of the state.[3]

The places and terms lingered, outcroppings of terror in public memory after the news grew stale. Love Canal, New York. Bhopal, India. Friendly Hills, Colorado, the "Love Canal West." Times Beach. Dioxin. PCBs. Agent Orange.

For many, it often seemed simply too overwhelming. Encouraged by the chemical industry, which had a vested self-interest in the widespread belief that "nothing can be done," people devised ways to avoid the thought that invisible danger from spreading poison might be hidden under the ground, in the drinking water, or in the food they eat. "Everything causes cancer," ran one common reaction. "Cancer is a risk that is part of modern society"—although, in fact, only 2 percent of chemicals are dangerous. Appealing to common sense, another message argued that "a little bit of anything is safe. Enough of anything can kill you." It often was presented with cartoons, showing rats overwhelmed by truckloads of saccharin. The reality turned out to be that, with some carcinogens, a little, any amount, can cause cancer; there are no "safe" levels. "The solution to cancer is to change your lifestyle," urged a third approach. Chemical industry experts argued that cancer rates in Charleston, West Virginia, might be due to higher rates of smoking in the city. When Weyerhauser timber company blanketed forests around Ashford, Washington, with Agent Orange, only two babies out of twelve were born alive in the town in the last half of 1979. The company sent Dr. Ilio Gauditz, a consultant, to a public meeting called to discuss the community's alarm. "Babies are replaceable," he told residents. He advised women to time pregnancies so as not to coincide with the spraying schedule.[4]

Spokespersons for the chemical industry argued that they were far more vigilant than any federal regulators ever could be. According to Geraldine Cox of the Chemical Manufacturers Association, the industry was "obsessed with safety, because of the nature of the product."[5]

The facts read like a litany of impending disasters. More than sixty thousand chemicals are in use, only 20 percent of which have even been tested according to minimum standards. An estimated six thousand companies and sites in the United States produce chemicals that may be hazardous or deadly, and 180,000 shipments of substances ranging from paint remover to nuclear waste are made each day by truck or rail. Each time we step on our car brake, asbestos fibers fill the air. The Environmental Protection Agency estimated that it would have to investigate more than twenty thousand sites as possible dangers to public health and place perhaps one tenth of them on the Superfund priority cleanup list. Outside observers called such figures conservative. The Congressional Office of Technology Assessment estimates that there are more than four hundred thousand dumps and that ten thousand would qualify for priority cleanup, at a cost of one hundred billion dollars.[6]

The threats worsened in the 1980s. Government regulations did not even cover carbamates, the kind of pesticides that include chemicals like Bhopal's MIC, as a hazard. One of the Reagan administration's first actions was to withdraw the Carter administration request that toxic chemicals in the workplace be identified. Policy under the direction of Environmental Protection Agency chief Anne Burford and her assistant Rita Lavelle, both of whom left office amid scandal, chose the least expensive course of action between potential victims' health care and the cost of cleanup. By 1985, the EPA had cleaned up only six toxic waste sites. "We've got no regulations and no enforcement," said Hugh Kaufman, an expert with the agency, describing dangers from tanks like those that leaked in Bhopal. "The only reason we haven't had a release with the same disastrous effect is that we've been lucky."[7]

On February 13, 1984, with simultaneous news conferences in Washington, D.C., and fifty-four other cities, a coalition of more than one hundred groups organized by Citizen Action and the Clean Water Action Project announced a nation-wide effort called the National Campaign Against Toxic Hazards. "The invasion of toxic chemicals into our bodies is America's No. 1 hidden health problem," said John O'Connor, coordinator of the effort. "People are frightened. People are angry. But more and more we are on the move to win new laws, to free us from toxic hazards. Politicians who deny us the tools for protection must be forced from office."[8]

Like a giant rousing from a numbness that was part fear, part hopelessness, the public had begun to take action to stem the mounting threat. The list of coalition participants included a mosaic of national organizations: the American Nurses Association, the Sierra Club, the National Council of Senior Citizens, the Interfaith Council for Protection of Animals and Nature, Citizens' Clearinghouse on Hazardous Waste, Silicon Valley Toxics Coalition, Congress Watch, the Consumer Federation of

America, the AFL-CIO, and the Izaak Walton League, among many others. But like the coalition around energy issues, the movement gained its force from local communities across the country.

O'Connor's own career reflected the forces coming together in Citizen Action and the National Campaign. O'Connor was a victim of the asbestos dumping in the community he grew up in and had seen several of his childhood friends die. That experience had moved him to join Massachusetts Fair Share as an organizer. After working to win important state laws, O'Connor became convinced of the need for a national effort and travelled the country building the national coalition.

For years, stories of personal hardship and disaster, often invisible to the public, had nonetheless been accumulating. "I lost two children. I want to keep that from happening to others," said Cathy Hinds of the Maine People's Alliance, blaming the death of one baby and the stillbirth of another on contamination from the McKin waste site in Gray, Maine, near her house. McKin, a deserted oil processing plant that poisoned wells in the area, had been placed on the EPA's emergency list in 1981, but little had been done. Five other sites in the state had already been identified as serious hazards, and sixty-eight additional sites were potentially dangerous. People from across the state called Hinds, founder of the Maine Citizens Coalition on Toxics, for advice. "People cry on the phone. One mother told me her child was born without a hand. I feel the pain. I ended up crying myself." In Center Point, Indiana, Carolina McCullough saw her dairy farm poisoned by dioxin. "The cows wouldn't eat. They would get down and wouldn't get up. They just rotted alive." Across the country, such stories multiplied, a grim and poignant counterpoint to environmental debates. But they also generated a grass roots movement, as more and more citizens, their backs to the wall, decided they had to do something themselves.[9]

Jean Pinard had grown up in the Ayer City neighborhood of Lowell, Massachusetts, and, after leaving the service and marrying his wife Rita, had moved back to the area in 1977, with their six-month-old daughter Rachel. Norine and Al Danley had lived in the community for several years. Phyllis Robey, a single mother, had moved in with her sister-in-law, not far away. Having left the Catholic church, in which she had grown up, because of the hypocrisy she saw between its professed values and its practice, she had not been active in much of anything. "I didn't even watch the news because it was so depressing," she remembered. "It was complete hopelessness. Nothing could be done. The big thing was what's for supper and what's on TV." [10]

In the late 1970s, the Pinards, the Danleys, and Robey all began to notice strange smells around the barrels in a nearby field. "Like a skunk outside," said Robey. Separately, they contacted city officials, who told them the smell was from a broken sewage line under the nearby street that road crews would fix when they had funds available. "Then I found out people all over the neighborhood were sick," recounted Jean Pinard. "You'd be walking and meet a neighbor with a baby in the carriage, ask how she was doing, and she'd say this is the fifth strep throat this winter. We started saying, 'This is crazy. What's going on?'" Noreen Danley had two miscarriages and another baby who died shortly after birth. Jean Pinard, a strong man who lifted weights for exercise, steadily lost weight and strength and was taken to the hospital.

In 1971 the Silresim Chemical Corporation operated a waste site facility in Ayer City that handled a variety of chemicals, from acids to ketone. In 1978, the state of Massachusetts passed a law "providing for the emergency removal of certain hazardous wastes in the City of Lowell" and commissioned a study, completed in 1979 but not made known to community residents, warning that Silresim had been cited repeatedly by the Massachusetts Division of Water Pollution Control. Violations included "unsatisfactory chemical handling procedures leading to soil contamination" from nearly thirty thousand drums of chemicals, acceptance of chemicals forbidden by law, and illegal discharge of waste into the municipal sewer system. Silresim's operating license had been revoked in late 1977, although a local bank, operating the company in receivership, continued to use the site for storage. After the state's emergency legislation, the Pollution Control Agency, finding that "the soil was permeated and the surface was characterized by colored pools, stains, evaporated residues and elastic gels," started to clean up the area but stopped when funds ran out. Meanwhile, Charlie Gargiulo, president of the chapter of Massachusetts Fair Share in the city, heard about the site. "'My God,' I thought, when we heard about it. 'Can this be real?' We checked it out. It was real."[11]

The community residents packed the meetings when Fair Share offered to help. "We'd go door to door with advice," Rita Pinard described, "telling people who they could go to see and who they could call. People would say, 'My God, so that's it,' and the puzzle pieces would fall into place." Phyllis Robey returned to the church when she found it taking action and became an expert on the similarities between Silresim and Love Canal. The Danleys travelled to meetings as far away as Washington, D.C. During the elections in 1982, Fair Share pressured then Governor King for six months and won promises that something would be done. But the governor failed to deliver. Many political observers credit Fair Share with having played a major role in defeating a conservative governor. Finally, as the new governor took office, the barrels were taken away. People's health improved immediately. But residents worried about long term effects of the contaminated soil. Although the site had been placed on the priority list of the EPA, federal officials had yet to take any action.[12]

Esla Bynoe-Andriolo, born in Jamaica and widely travelled, was fluent in languages and taught linguistics at Jersey City University in New Jersey. She had long been involved in choral groups, and her choir had sung at Rockefeller Plaza and the United Nations. But she had always shied away from what she described as "civic affairs" until an organizer for a citizen group, ACORN, knocked at her door. "Out of politeness I had to invite him in," she recalled with a laugh. When she went to a community meeting the next Monday, Bynoe-Andriolo met about thirty residents of the neighborhood for the first time, although she had lived there two years. "It was a very conservative area, with many Republicans. I was the only black." But Bynoe-Andriolo, elected chair, led the community in its successful efforts to gain more police protection, do something about landlords, and address other issues. The experience taught her the value of organizing. "I said, 'My God, people have this tool and they don't use it.' We got results. And I felt 1,000 percent more involved in the community."[13]

Bynoe-Andriolo got the ACORN chapters throughout Jersey City to affiliate with New Jersey Citizen Action when the organization formed in 1983. The state group, along with New Jersey Clean Water, an activist environmental group, proved invaluable allies in a campaign to clean up the PJP dump site (known by the initials of the previous land owners), not far from where she lived.

"At the first meeting when we brainstormed about community problems, someone had listed PJP," she recalled. There was good reason. Acrid smoke from the area drifted across the neighborhoods. Flare-ups and explosions occurred continually. Concrete piles from a bridge that stood on the site were corroding. The incidence of cancer, respiratory ailments, and other health problems in the area was high. Although Bynoe-Andriolo's instincts were to be cautious about making any accusations, the situation seemed to her dangerous. When the neighborhood got the EPA report that listed PJP as a priority for cleanup, it was the final straw. "We demanded the mayor form a task force, and he asked me to head it. I decided the only way to have clout was to have community leaders and scientists and city officials all together." The mayor served, as did the city lawyer, the head of the city Health Department, the fire chief, and the director of Engineering.

Earl (Tex) Aldridge, head of the city's Environmental Task Force, who walks with a cane as the result of a Vietnam War injury, made a trek to the state capital, Trenton, to draw attention to the site. "It's the only way we're going to open the ears of the politicians," he explained. Then in the spring of 1985, fifteen hundred residents rallied in Lincoln Park across from PJP. Politicians gave speeches. Banners and signs from communities across the city fluttered in the air. Then, the crowd turning solemn and quiet, a man dug a hole. They planted a tree, to symbolize life. And they dedicated it to a woman who had just died of cancer, who had lived three hundred yards away.

It all had effect. Thomas Kean, governor of the state, allocated ten million dollars for cleanup. The state Department of Health agreed to do a screening for health problems. And the residents of Jersey City joined with other communities throughout the state in a successful campaign for the strongest state "right-to-know" bill that would require companies to provide a list of hazardous chemicals being used in the workplace and stored in communities. Indeed, passage of the bill was a dramatic turnaround. In January of 1983, when the right-to-know legislation was tied up in committee, chemical industry spokespersons had bragged that they would stop the spreading movement for right-to-know legislation in New Jersey.

As the fights in Lowell and Jersey City suggested, some important victories could be won on local and state levels. By the summer of 1985, more than sixty local communities and thirty states had passed right-to-know legislation in campaigns most often organized by affiliates of Citizen Action. A few states had followed the lead of Connecticut, which had enacted a ban on landfills of toxic waste. Others had established state cleanup funds on their own. But the problem was nation-wide in scope, solvable in a long term sense only by concerted federal action and national resources. It was clear enough to community residents across the country that they needed to band together in a national effort, if the dangers from toxic waste were to be lessened.

In 1980, spurred in part by the revelations about Love Canal, Congress passed the Comprehensive Environmental Response, Compensation, and Liability Act—commonly known as the Superfund bill—with the stated purpose of protecting public health and the environment from poisonous wastes and toxic substances. It mandated a program of $1.6 billion to be used by the Environmental Protection Agency, which was to begin cleanups immediately. A small portion of funding for the program, about 12.5 percent, came from general federal revenues. Other sources depended upon taxes that would be levied on chemical materials, and, in particular, those responsible for toxic pollution would be ordered to pay fees to help with cleanup.[14]

The National Priority List, or NPL, contained the sites that the EPA identified as the most serious threats to health and safety. Once a site appears on the NPL, it qualified for what the EPA called "remedial action," designed to remove the danger. By 1985, 850 sites were on the list. Yet from the beginning, the effort was plagued by bureaucratic inertia and scandal. After five years, long term cleanup had still not begun at more than 90 percent of the sites. And, although the EPA once claimed that six had been cleaned up, it now acknowledged that none had really been—as a result of studies by the National Campaign Against Toxic Hazards that exposed how superficial and incomplete those cleanup efforts had been.

The National Campaign Against Toxic Hazards in 1985 fought for a number of changes in the Superfund to make it more effective. It sought an increase in funding to $10.1 billion over the next five years. It proposed mandatory cleanup schedules for the EPA and strict standards for cleanup procedures that would bring sites into compliance with environmental quality guidelines. It demanded that polluting companies continue to be liable for costs of cleanup, that victims be allowed to sue for damages, and that the national law contain an effective right-to-know standard that did not preempt stronger local and state laws.

Yet the Reagan administration and the chemical industry strenuously opposed all these measures and sought to weaken the existing legislation. In an early victory, they succeeded in moving legislation out of the Congressional Subcommittee on Commerce, Tourism, and Transportation that would have pre-empted community right-to-know laws with a watered-down federal law. Cathy Hurwit, a former congressional staffer, as legislative director for Citizen Action negotiated the lobbying with skill connecting the grass roots to the Hill. The threatened federal legislation would allow storage facilities to decide what new chemicals to list, without any independent reviewing procedure; permit such facilities to exempt poisonous materials declared "trade secrets," without any mechanism to challenge the claim; and remove any requirements for reporting to citizens on the discharges of hazardous chemicals into the air, water, or soil. The stage was set for a bitter battle.[15]

In North Carolina, where affiliates of the National Campaign Against Toxic Hazards included groups from the Carolina Community Project and Clean Water Action Fund to the League of Women Voters and the Sierra Club, participants in the campaign held simultaneous press conferences in Charlotte, Raleigh, Greensboro, and Fayetteville to ask Senators Jesse Helms and John East to vote for more money for cleanup. Illinois Public Action charged that Senator Charles Percy had received $132,000 from sixty-five manufacturing companies that were involved in the production of toxic chemicals, pointing out that the senator had voted against a 1982 amendment to Superfund that would have provided additional funds and supported the removal of cancer-causing asbestos from schools. Idaho Fair Share similarly revealed that Representative Larry Craig had received funds from chemical industries' political action committees. Rhode Island CLOC pressured their senator John Chafee to take leadership to make sure the pollutors and not the consumers would pay for toxic waste cleanup. In Washington, Fair Share criticized both Republican senators for holding up reauthorization of the Superfund. In Florida, Karen Clarke, director of the Citizen Action affiliated Florida Consumer Federation, pointed out that, even where federal action had been taken to clean up sites, it was insufficient. "The tanks were drained in Temple Terrace," she said, describing a site called Tri-City Oil, "but they weren't cleaned. So you still have fumes and people complaining about headaches." Federal officials of the EPA, though disagreeing with many specific criticisms of the National Campaign, often conceded a central point. "They're right," said Russ Dawson, a spokesman for the agency. "We don't have enough money." [16]

In more than two hundred congressional districts across the country, the fight over Superfund had been made an issue in the 1984 elections, often with powerful effect. Many opponents of increases in funding for federal cleanup switched their positions. Some, like Charles Percy, lost to challengers.

The canvass played a key role. In 1984, more than twelve million homes were contacted about toxic waste and the fight for Superfund. Throughout 1985, battles around state right-to-know legislation added to the pressure on Washington politicians as well. The climax of the campaign to fight for a reauthorized and strengthened national effort came in the fall, as the "Super Drive" brought the heartland to the nation's capital, with graphic evidence. [17]

From the four corners of the nation, trucks converged on Washington through September, 1985. Community coalitions and Citizen Action chapters sent delegations that represented the enormity of the problem of toxic wastes and the breadth of the movement alike: Oregon. California. Idaho. Colorado. Minnesota. Iowa. Illinois. Indiana. Ohio. Maine. New Hampshire. Massachusetts. New York. Connecticut. New Jersey. Pennsylvania. Maryland. Virginia. Florida. Alabama. They brought samples of air and water taken from toxic waste sites and symbols of injury and disease that resulted from the poisons. Some pictures drawn by children even reflected humor in the midst of calamity. "It's no fun being #1," ran the headline on one, with a miserable duck lamenting that his home had been named "the #1 Toxic Waste Site in U.S.A." Another proclaimed a new logo for the movement: "Dumpbusters," with a crossed out skull and barrels of poison. Along with such evidence, moreover, came a demonstration of enormous power: signatures collected from 1.5 million American citizens, demanding that Congress take effective action. The halls of Congress received a message that had never been imagined by the nation's founders.[18]

It had effect. "The climate on the Hill has been completely changed from a year ago," noted one Washington observer. As the fight around Superfund came to a climax, all the major media followed the story, and *Time* magazine's cover story on October 14 was "Toxic Wastes: The Poisoning of America '85." The Senate, which had refused to pass a bill to renew Superfund at the level of $6 billion in 1984, sent to the House a funding authorization at the level of $7.5 billion. The industry and administration effort to insert weak right-to-know provisions that would pre-empt local communities' stronger legislation was turned on its head: the Superfund legislation passed by both houses of Congress contained strong right-to-know provisions, which allowed local communities to pass stronger legislation yet. "We have a far bigger problem than anyone thought," conceded Lee Thomas, the third director of the scandal-ridden Environmental Protection Agency under the Reagan administration. "There are far more sites that are far more difficult to deal with than anybody ever anticipated." The Superfund bill also included mandatory cleanup schedules, a long sought goal of the movement.[19]

On many fronts, the war against toxic hazards would continue into the future. Only legislation sharply reducing the amounts of toxic hazards being produced by American industries each year and limiting the methods of disposal would seriously "solve" the problem of the enormous, deadly threats. As the *Time* cover story concluded, "In the end, only a vast effort by the industries that profit from the chemicals can get the waste mess under control." [20]

With the renewal and strengthening of the Superfund law by the House and Senate, the National Campaign Against Toxic Hazards had achieved its first, critical goal. They still are vigilant against political upsets that might overturn this progress. Looking to the future, the Campaign began to broaden its focus. Superfund provides for cleanup of dumping that has already occurred but does not touch the problems being created by the mountains of toxic chemicals produced and disposed of each day.

The National Campaign Against Toxic Hazards is working to develop a comprehensive solution to all toxic hazards. This solution includes better pretesting of chemicals; a source reduction system to reduce toxic wastes; developing safe substitutes to the dangerous waste intensive products of the petrochemical industry; a chemical accident prevention program for potential Bhopals; and strengthened legal rights for victims. In short, the campaign aims to transform the chemical industry so that the country's manufacture, use, and disposal of the worst toxic substances is substantially reduced.

In 1986 and beyond, these grass roots toxic groups will be working to enforce cleanup laws and get responsible parties to prevent toxic wastes. Several Citizen Action organizations have already won state laws banning the disposal of hazardous wastes in landfills. Those campaigns will now be waged in other states as well. In many areas, organizations will work for state laws to discourage the generation of toxic waste. And these organizations will work to ensure that Superfund is used to clean up the most dangerous waste sites in America, quickly and effectively.

Much, in sum, remained to be done. But the victories and the public attention also evidenced the growing power of grass roots citizen organizing. They also raised broader questions about basic American values and purposes. In the mid-eighties, the plight of rural America similarly brought to the forefront of public discussion the most fundamental issues of what the nation stands for, and where it is going.

7. HARD TIMES ON THE FARM

Standing by the auction man
Taking bids on her land
Grandma looked down at her hands
Drier than the soil
Penny here, nickel there
Celebration filled the air
Grandma raised her eyes in prayer
Thankful for that day
When the auctioneer was done
The country folk they had won
Without spilling any blood
That saved the family farm.

Larry Long, "Grandma's Penny Sale," *Run for Freedom*

People in rural America don't talk much about their problems in public. "When you're on a tractor all day by yourself, you get to be a good philosopher, but you don't tell your story to anyone. You just personalize it," explained Anne Kanten, a founder of the American Agriculture Movement, who later served as assistant commissioner of agriculture in Minnesota. "It's a battle between you and the land. It challenges your ingenuity. And what you do seems on display. You're compared with the farmer across the street. You sit around the coffee shop and talk about how many bushels you're going to harvest. But nobody knows what you talk about to your banker." Wabasha County, in south-eastern Minnesota, would seem a case in point.[1]

Virtually untouched by the waves of earlier rural protest that had broken across the state periodically, Wabasha is rockribbed Republican territory, a most unlikely place for anything that smacks of what people around there call "political activism." The terrain is wrinkled like some ancient, weathered face of a giant, with rocky bluffs along the Mississippi River, rolling hills and ravines, and thick forests of fir and cedar. German immigrants, settling in the nineteenth century, found it difficult to farm large areas, but they dotted the land with neat dairy barns and fields of feed grain. And they created closeknit, conservative Catholic communities that seemed for decades impervious to change.

Joanne Klees grew up on a dairy farm in the eastern part of the county near the Mississippi. Assertive and adventurous, Klees left the area for several years after graduating from high school in 1974. She travelled with her sister to Europe, worked on farms in Israel and Norway, picked oranges in Florida, spent some time in Maine. When she came back in 1983, things had begun to change dramatically. "Neighbors used to work together. A family would cut the grain itself, but other families would join for the actual thrashing of the grain. One would have the thrasher and another the binder, but people also did it because they enjoyed getting together." But economic conditions had begun to force major alterations in social patterns. Family farm income in 1978 had averaged $35,174. In 1982 it averaged $11,692. By 1984, it had plummeted to just $6,000. "People have had to get bigger and bigger just to get by. There's not time to get together anymore. People are in the fields on Sunday now. I've seen headlights out in the fields at 2 A.M."[2]

In 1985, Carolyn Slocum, an organizer for the citizen action group Minnesota Citizens Organizations Acting Together—COACT, for short —helped Klees and her friend Marge Warthesen organize a meeting to talk about farm problems. They called others and sent out notices through local church bulletins—Catholic parishes, especially, had been discussing the farm crisis for several years. "I was unsure how people would react," said Klees. "People around here are real skeptical of politics." But over sixty people showed up. They decided to found a county chapter of a new organization in Minnesota called Groundswell. It immediately had impact. "We did a news conference," remembered Klees. "I ended up speaking for the first time into a camera. I'm used to being real discreet in Wabasha County. When you show up on the news, it's not discreet. But everywhere I go people tell me, 'Gee, we're glad people are doing something.'" When a legislator came to a local meeting of Groundswell, he got angry when he heard the farmers complaining about Republican policies. And people were furious in response. "That's been the subject of talk for two months now. He didn't respect people, and he yelled at a local constituent. You don't do that. We told him he owed his office to us." [3]

In the winter of 1985, the mood was bleak throughout rural America. "Partly it's a feeling of desolation," Kanten described. "You find farm families who won't even answer the phone." Suicide calls to the Southwestern Mental Health Center in Luverne, Minnesota, ran almost 25 percent more than the year before. But alongside despair, a movement had begun to gather momentum in every rural region of the country, involving people like Joanne Klees and Marge Warthesen. [4]

By the early months of 1985, news of the farm crisis was carried front page across the country. CBS Evening News featured stories of farm protesters and members of the new Congressional Populist Caucus like Tom Harkin planting 250 white crosses in a park across from the White House, as a memorial to the number of farmers going out of business each day. Minnesota Groundswell's winter rally closed thirty-four school districts in the state and brought more than seventeen thousand farmers to the state capitol in St. Paul. In South Dakota, the new Farm Crisis Committee resulted in 103 of the 105 state representatives travelling to Washington, D.C., to lobby on behalf of farming communities. To the tune of "Home on the Range," a crowd in Sylvester, Georgia, sang protest songs as they gathered to block the foreclosure of a farm. *U.S. News and World Report*, headlining "Farmers Up in Arms," reported that "in one of the most massive and well-organized lobbying efforts since the height of protests against the Vietnam War, thousands of farmers, small-town bankers and other rural residents called for emergency funds to keep many among an estimated 430,000 financially desperate food producers from going under."[5]

The farm movement embarrassed the Reagan administration, fresh from its victory in November among just those farm belt constituencies like Wabasha, which had been stalwart Republican strongholds for generations. Yet the issues were not likely to soon go away. In seven midwestern states, more than 20 percent of farmers had acquired debts equal to at least 40 percent of their assets in 1985. In more than thirty other states, 15 percent or more of the farm population faced a similar problem. And 1986 was worse yet. Moreover, the farmers most in trouble were often those who, in the early 1970s, saw interest rates only 1 or 2 percent over inflation. In those years, according to David Harrington, an economist with the Agriculture Department, "They were the young aggressive go-getters, the best managers. It seemed a wise, even conservative, use of resources to allow debt up to 30 percent of assets." A study by the government's Office of Technology Assessment, released in March of 1985, warned that technological and economic changes threatened the existence of mid-sized farms over the next fifteen years. The crisis, moreover, was far broader than the numbers of farmers directly affected. "No country can ever be free without a strong landed constituency and widespread land ownership," argued Anne Kanten. "It's not a farm crisis, it's a crisis of the whole country." The historical evidence reinforced her warnings.'[6]

In the 1940s, Walter Goldschmidt, a researcher for the Department of Agriculture, conducted detailed studies of two California towns, Arvin and Dinuba. The towns had roughly equivalent levels of agricultural production in terms of dollar value. But they differed widely in size of farms. Dinuba had many small, family oriented units. Arvin was made of a few giant producers.[7]

Goldschmidt found that the communities differed radically along many dimensions. As Frances Moore Lappé and Joseph Collins summarized in their book *Food First*, Dinuba supported:

About 20 percent more people and at a higher level of income
A working population that was mostly self-employed in contrast to

the large-farm community where less than 20 percent were self-
employed—and nearly two thirds were agricultural wage laborers
Many more democratic decision making organizations and much
broader representation in them
Better schools, and more parks, newspapers, civic groups, churches,
and public services
Twice the number of small businesses and 61 percent more retail
business

When researchers returned to the two towns in the late 1970s, they discovered that the contrasts had become even sharper. In 1945, Dinuba, the
small farm community, had a median family income 12 percent higher
than that in Arvin. By the 1970s, it had grown to 28 percent.[8]

Along with the demise of family farms, in short, came the collapse of
a way of life, from local feed grain stores, grain elevators, and lumber
yards to the local school and church. "From 1981 to 1983, we saw a
tremendous washout of businesses," said John Lee, administrator of the
Agriculture Department's Economic Research Service. "Particularly on
the Main Streets of small towns." By the mid-eighties, whole communities throughout the nation's agricultural regions began to feel like ghost
towns. But the impact was not the result of the workings of the "free
market," as administration officials were wont to claim—and some liberals, urging accommodation to supposedly "inevitable change," were
wont to agree. Rather, they were the result of more than a generation of
federal agricultural policies.[9]

Walter Goldschmidt, the Department of Agriculture researcher, had
planned to study a number of other farming communities as well. But
the department quickly ordered him to stop any further research. The
reason was not hard to fathom. His studies proved a dramatic embar-
rassment to department policy.

Throughout the forties, fifties, and sixties, federal agricultural policies
had largely reflected the interests and views of large farmers and grain
corporations. Indeed, the positions of the upper levels of the Department of Agriculture were customarily filled with executives from the
large grain companies. And those executives had a specific agenda: they

sought to increase the size of farms, decrease the prices of farm produce, and drive large numbers of family farmers off the land. Thus, for instance, the 1962 report on agriculture of the Committee for Economic Development, a "who's who" of corporate figures urged the "moving off the farm of about two million of the present farm labor force." To accomplish such ends, the CED recommended that "the price supports for wheat, cotton, rice, feed grains and related crops now under price supports be reduced immediately." In 1974 in a follow-up report, the CED found, to its gratification, that "in general, policies of this nature have been pursued by the U.S. government." [10]

In the early 1970s, federal policies escalated the dangers to the nation's family farmers. The Nixon administration, panicked about a growing trade deficit, determined that large scale food exports would aid in the balance of payment crisis and prove a useful tool in foreign policy as well. It called its new plan Food Power. Government officials encouraged increased farm production, promising to aid in the sale of grain and other produce overseas through generous subsidies to overseas purchasers, an undervalued dollar, and extension of credit to foreign governments. But exports were not controlled by farmers or the government. Six giant grain dealers made up 85 percent of all U.S. grain trade. And government policies dramatically favored the corporations. In the winter of 1971–72, a wave of extreme cold and snow killed twenty-five million acres of wheat in the Soviet Union, equalling the total U.S. acreage of wheat. It was clear that the Soviets would make an enormous purchase of American grains. But the Department of Agriculture, legally required to inform farmers of its knowledge of any upcoming sales, instead warned that there would be a large surplus that year. By June, 1972, Continental Grain, Cargil, and other large exporters made offers to buy the harvest early. What farmers knew was that their harvest would be large. They did not know that the Soviets were preparing to buy. Grain dealers bought wheat at $1.25 a bushel. A few weeks later, the same produce sold for $2.25, and the following year it reached $5.00. Not until mid-July did the department reveal its information. Earl Butz, secretary of agriculture, later responded to criticisms by saying the grain companies won in the situation because "farmers weren't smart enough to take advantage of the situation." He neglected to mention that Clarence Palmby, the official who had arranged the largest grain purchase in history, left his post at the Department of Agriculture to become vice president of Continental Grain, the company that signed the agreement.[11]

Despite manipulation, farm income in the early seventies, buoyed by new markets, rose. Many young people went into farming; others took out loans and expanded their operations. Farm lands skyrocketed in value, fueled in part by a rush of speculation. But the incentives to increase constantly in size and volume of produce laid grounds for future crises, at home and abroad.

In poor and developing Third World nations, the result of Food Power often was to sell large quantities of grain at or below world market prices. Very little reached the very poor. Moreover, the purchases of imported food at prices that were lower than small farmers could afford to match undermined domestic production. Millions of peasants, reacting to such pressures, left the land in the 1970s and streamed into teaming Third World ghettoes.[12]

Domestically, in the longer term, pressures to expand undermined the careful husbandry of the land that farmers most often wanted to practice. "Butz's policy was to plant fence post to fence post," Joanne Klees of Wabasha County remembered. "It's not that farmers thought getting bigger was better. We thought that's how we have to make it. That's when conservation went to pot. All the pasture land went under production." There were more immediate worries. The increase in production, the growing debt of farmers, the speculation of land values—all pointed to a collapse in the not far distant future, as increases in prices that farmers received for farm goods increasingly lagged behind the costs of production.[13]

From 1978 on, real prices of agricultural commodities started to decline steadily. By 1982, average prices were below the all-time low, breaking the records of the Great Depression years. In 1983, prices were still lower. In the period from 1980 through 1985, farm production costs alone exceeded the total farm income.[14]

When the crisis hit, moreover, family farmers suffered the worst, despite the fact that study after study has shown such units to be the most productive. Benefits of government programs had gone to the largest producers: in 1982, 70 percent went to the largest 10 percent of the farmers. Tax structures were created primarily to aid larger businesses. And family farms, with less diversification, were less able to survive through extended losses.[15]

It was out of this crisis that a new farm movement swept across rural America by 1984. But its roots were several years earlier. The tractorcade to Washington in the winter of 1978 sponsored by the American Agriculture Movement had been a harbinger of increased activism. In states like Kansas and Missouri, strong AAM networks continued to do advocacy, direct action, and voter registration. In a number of states, new organizations like the Iowa Farm Unity Coalition and Prairiefire joined with older groups like the National Farmers Organization and the Farmers Union in midwestern states to seek legislation that would halt foreclosures of farms, help farmers negotiate with lenders, and fight for more reasonable pricing policies. "Where you had a credible organization or coalition develop, like in Iowa, people have been able to take advantage of the movement that spontaneously emerged in 1985," observed Becky Glass of the Youth Project, a resource and technical assistance center that works with many farm groups. In states like Minnesota, Illinois, Ohio, and Indiana, Citizen Action affiliates played key roles in helping lay the groundwork for future movement.[16]

Minnesota Citizens Organizations Acting Together, or COACT, had begun work on policies of the Farm Home Administration in 1980 in Little Falls. FmHA, a federally created agency, is supposed to be the lender of last resort. Farmers with FmHA loans were often poor or young farmers with lower equity. Thus they were the first to feel the pressures. Moreover, despite FmHA's mandate to service struggling farmers, in many areas the agency seemed arbitrary and inaccessible. From Little Falls, COACT expanded farm work into a state-wide campaign, trying to make FmHA more responsible. The organization had a series of demands—that local county committees have more control over the FmHA supervisors, that farmers be notified of policies, that they have access to files, and others—and had several victories. But organizing in rural areas was slow, hampered by the strong reluctance of farmers to talk about their individual situations. COACT concentrated on public events. On August 26, 1982, it brought back the tactic of "Penny Auctions" to prevent foreclosures.[17]

Farmers gathered at the home of a young farm family, the Conans, who were being forced off their land, determined to convince potential buyers not to bid anything higher than a nickel or a dollar. The auctioneer called off the sale. And the organization helped the farmers negotiate a deal with the FmHA state director to refinance the farm and resume operations. In Payneville, Minnesota, COACT sent a negotiating team into the office of a local bank president, carrying the proposals of the Catholic bishop of the diocese, George Speltz, for resolving a crisis on the Conans' farm. The bank called in the police, and a caravan of sheriff cars drove the group away. "The sheriff was sympathetic," remembered Joe Chrastil, the coordinator of COACT's farm organizing. "He asked the county to purchase a bus because he thought this was going to happen a lot."

In addition to the specific problems, all such public events helped make the point that the growing economic problems that people experienced were not theirs alone. "People would sit around the kitchen table and we would say, 'This is happening all over. Everybody has troubles. If your banker tells you that you're the only one it's a lie,'" Chrastil described. A hot line that farmers could call for information and advice turned out to be a striking success. "People could call anonymously. And we were flooded with calls from all over the state." Carolyn Slocum, organizing in the conservative southeast sections of the state, found it even harder to organize people. "Very rarely would I run into anyone who had organizing experience," she remembered. "I would try to draw people out, get them to talk about their own situation, realize there was a general problem."[18]

Steady organizing over several years established a network of leaders around the state. Then in 1984, the mood shifted. "It was very dramatic," Slocum recounted. "Suddenly, people realized they're not the only ones." When Bobbi Polzine, a rural activist and COACT member in Brewster, called a meeting in October and hundreds showed up, including local business leaders and professionals, the impact was felt across the state. It swiftly coalesced into the organization Groundswell, which brought thousands to the state capitol in the winter to demand a moratorium on foreclosures for a year and minimum grain price legislation. COACT threw its organizing staff into service of the movement. "The number of counties I covered went from four to twenty," Slocum described. "We'd set up a dozen chairs and 120 people would show up."[19]

As the farm crisis spread, it attracted support from many other arenas. Entertainers, especially country and western singers many of whom had their own roots on farms, sang of the farmer's plight. Willie Nelson, the "outlaw" poet of America's heartland, came to their assistance. He organized Farm Aid, a massive concert drawing entertainers and audiences across the country, to raise funds that were distributed to many of the self-help efforts of the farm groups.

Out of the farm organizing, with aid from political figures like Jim Hightower of Texas and Tom Harkin of Iowa and organizers like Mark Ritchie of the League of Rural Voters, farmers developed what was called "the populist alternative" to the Reagan policies and traditional farm subsidy programs alike. The bill was the Farm Policy Reform Act of 1985, or simply "the Harkin Bill." Its fundamental aim was to increase the power of family farmers in dealing with lending institutions and commodity purchasers. It included several main features:

> Elimination of subsidy payments. Under the act, producers would receive a fair price for crops from buyers, not from government. The price floor would be set initially at roughly the full cost of production —30 percent higher than 1985 prices. Incremental rises in price floors over the next ten years would bring prices to the level at which farmers' returns on equity were roughly equivalent to the rest of the economy.
> Balancing production with need. Farmers enrolling in the program would vote on mandatory production controls to limit production of storable commodities to actual demand, domestically and internationally, so as not to generate the enormous surpluses that were devastating farm life.
> Benefits would be targeted specifically for family farms.
> Conservation practices would be encouraged, including the creation

of a Conservation Reserve for highly erodible land, taken out of row-crop production.

Increased funding for humanitarian food aid and domestic food programs would be made available.

Aid in restructuring debt and credit would be given.

By the fall of 1985, the National Save the Family Farm Committee, formed to lobby for the bill, provided a coordinating center for the growing movement. The committee included groups that ranged from Illinois Farm Alliance to the Federation of Southern Cooperatives. The administration was fiercely opposed to the bill. Reagan officials charged it would dramatically increase the cost of food to consumers—even though the reality was that the cost of a loaf of bread would rise no more than three or four cents. And the administration sought, instead, to increase production still more, driving out smaller farmers and aggressively undercutting other nations' production. "You can still make a small fortune in farming today, but you gotta start with a large one," quipped Jim Hightower, Secretary of Agriculture in Texas.

In longer range terms, organizers drew on ideas like those developed by the Family Farm Resource Center. Any federal benefits, according to the center, should be carefully targeted to family sized farmers. Diversified farming—more economically stable, labor intensive, and far more conserving of natural resources—should be encouraged. Extensive soil conservation and stewardship programs should be developed. Federal and state legislation should give communities far more control over the use of money generated in their areas. Federal guidelines, for instance, might require certain levels of local reinvestment, establish standards for loan eligibility, and prescribe application of loan servicing options to be implemented before anyone could lose title to farm or home.

In the face of intransigent opposition from the Reagan administration and corporate interests alike, organizers in the movement foresaw several years of battling. But once again, the techniques and methods pioneered by the new citizen movements were proving of use. In October, 1985, a combined canvass by Groundswell and Minnesota COACT opened in Silbey County, Minnesota, with canvassers staying in the homes of local farm leaders. Organizers in the movement believed this communications tool held great promise for mobilizing and educating rural America on a massive scale.[20]

Meanwhile, fear and despair in America's rural communities were also breeding reaction. As Merle Hansen, president of the North American Farm Alliance, put it, "When people are being torn by their roots, they look for someone to blame." White supremacy and extreme right wing groups urged farmers to stop paying taxes, resist courts, and arm themselves. "To put it simply," proclaimed an Open Letter to the American Farmer, "the Jew plan is to steal your land!" It appeared in the Ku Klux Klan publication *White Patriot*, which taught that Jews are children of the devil. But often right wing efforts were more insidious. "Groups like the Klan have learned how to dress in jeans, boots, and a baseball cap instead of white robes, speak the farmer's language, and offer to help save the farm," recounted Dan Levitas of the Iowa Farm Unity Coalition, which monitors such groups. The newspaper of a new group calling itself the Populist Party claimed a circulation of several hundred thousand, mainly from rural areas. It vehemently denied any racial or religious bigotry. But both publication and party, according to the Anti-Defamation League of B'nai B'rith, were creations of Willis Carto, founder of the Liberty Lobby and prominent anti-Semitic ideologue.[21]

Responding to the agricultural crisis, a group with increasingly sophisticated organizing efforts, rooted in local communities and coordinating their work on state, regional, and national levels as well, sought to channel the discontent into effective and progressive political directions. "We are competing every day for the ear of farmers who are now becoming politically aware for the first time because of the problems they are facing," said Joe Chrastil, director of the Family Farm Organizing Resource Center, which began out of the work of COACT. Allan Libbra, founder of Illinois Public Action's Illinois Farm Alliance, a group whose work had closely paralleled that of its sister Citizen Action affiliate, COACT, foresaw possibilities for far ranging political change in rural communities as a result of the crisis. "If the times are good for nothing else, they're good for that," he said with some bitterness. "My view is that a 20 percent realignment in rural areas is doable." Some conservatives made much the same point. "The political payoff of the farm belt financial crisis may be a reverse party realignment," worried Rowland Evans and Robert Novak in the *Washington Post* in 1985. "While still high nationwide, Ronald Reagan is in deep trouble in his native Midwestern heartland."[22]

More than money or particular political fortunes were at stake. In the near term, the survival of a way of life in rural America based on the family farm was on the line. The longer range questions were who controls the land and who shapes America's future. These questions would be fought out in communities across the country—and settled, finally, in the nation's capital.

8. POPULIST POLITICS

*As my Daddy used to say, there's nothing in the middle
of the road but yellow stripes and dead armadillos.*

Jim Hightower,
Texas Secretary of Agriculture

Galesburg is an old railroad and manufacturing town of thirty-five thousand in western Illinois. It seems an unlikely location for a political earthquake. Once Galesburg had been a way station for the "underground railroad," a place where slaves escaping from the South could find lodging and refuge. But since those days, the area had settled into a pattern that seemed the essence of predictability. Republicans had won every election for Congress but one since the Civil War. Groups like the Farm Bureau, the National Rifle Association, and the Veterans of Foreign Wars set the political tone. This was conservative, rural mid-America, not far from Ronald Reagan's hometown, knit together by voluntary fire departments and the Saturday church social. Thus, it came as something of a shock to outside political observers when a thirty-one-year-old activist legal aid attorney named Lane Evans won the election to Congress as an outspoken Democratic opponent of the president in 1982. Over the next two years, the fact that Evans continually increased his popularity in the district, while he simultaneously compiled the most anti-Reagan voting record in the House of Representatives, proved even more startling. From the point of view in Evans's district, however, it made perfect sense. According to Chuck Hudnall, manager of a manufacturing company in town, Evans was "a straight shooter" who was "representing a cross section of people." The Republican mayor of Galesburg, Jerry Miller, added that "people from both parties are impressed" with Evans. "He's established a strong base." [1]

Growing unemployment from factory shutdowns in towns like Galesburg and neighboring Moline and Rock Island had combined with hardship among farmers to stir up political trouble in the 1980s. But President Reagan remained popular in the district even among those who had lost jobs or farms. People farther to the right, backed by lavish financial resources, sought to organize the discontent that existed. In the Republican primary of 1982, an ultraconservative state senator, Kenneth McMillan, beat the incumbent moderate Republican congressman, Tom Railsback. The key to the political revolution wrought by Lane Evans was not a change in the district's political coloration. Evans's strength was his populist appeal. He championed supposedly "conservative" social values like community, family, faith, hard work, and patriotism — precisely the themes that had been the rhetorical mainstay of Ronald Reagan — but in a way that reinterpreted the threat and the solution. "We're against the big corporations," Evans explained, "[but] you'll see populists fight for small banks and savings and loans. The real problem is the lack of social fabric in the country due to centralization." In these terms, Evans spoke to the sense of dislocation wrought by an economy and government that seemed increasingly out of control. He had argued that "most people are underrepresented in both parties." And, pointing to his successes and those of the other members of the Congressional Populist Caucus he had helped to found in 1983, he disagreed with those Democrats who maintained the party had to become more cautious. "We have to learn from the elections," Evans argued. "But we can't learn the wrong lesson. Becoming Republicans won't help. We have to get back to fundamentals and identify the new coalition of farmers, small business, workers and others who are not being considered by the federal government at this point." [2]

Evans, friendly and down to earth, listens carefully to people. The large number of voters in the district who pulled levers for Evans and Reagan alike in 1984 is part testimony to his careful work of constituency service (his staff operates from four centers and a travelling office) that reflects his attentiveness. Evans's success reflects an emerging political change in the 1980s. Evans, like many other successful progressive populists, combines an effective appeal and strong leadership with sophisticated techniques of voter mobilization and grass roots organizing, developed by citizen groups like Illinois Public Action Council, on whose state board he sits. Thus, Evans's presence in Congress represents a new phenomenon in the 1980s: a generation of progressive political leadership closely tied to the new forms of citizen organizing. Indeed, there have been an increasing number of signs throughout the decade that this political movement will prove a potent, successful alternative to populism from the right. The new populist electoral action is seen not as a substitute for ongoing organizing that empowers ordinary citizens but as a tactic that can aid the process. As Lynn Cardiff of Oregon Fair Share puts it, "We know we should not tie ourselves to any politician's career. And we know we need organizations of average citizens. But elections are part of the process of gaining a voice."[3]

In the 1984 elections, populism made its appearance with apparent suddenness, as pundits and news commentators all began to notice the success of political appeals to a widespread public sentiment of powerlessness that did not fit easily into normal political equations. But behind the visible signs of populism was a much longer history of effective organizing on the right, on the one hand, and among progressive citizen organizations, on the other.

For many years, the new right movement had gained power, using "a political language that was strongly value based," as Michael Ansara, Massachusetts Fair Share founding director and an initiator of Citizen Action, put it. By the mid-eighties, Reagan administration officials were labelling the mood they appealed to as "populism." Richard Darman, deputy secretary of the Treasury, argued that contemporary populism— which he defined as "anti-elitist, opposed to excessive concentrations of power, oriented toward fairness and toward a degree of levelling"—was "broader than may conventionally be recognized. It extends beyond stereotypical 'blue-collar' and 'red-neck' America—well into the vast world of the white collars . . . the ones who have made it to white-collar clothes but not to Yuppie power or position." According to Darman, these workers are America's "legions of quiet populists," almost 55 percent of the workforce, "only a small fraction of [whom] have 'made it.'" Most "live lives of frustrated hopes . . . a quiet con game." They "have changed clothes [but] not significantly changed their place." And they know all too well that "things haven't turned out as expected."[4]

New Right populists sought to channel the discontents of the American middle class through what might be called a politics of powerlessness, pointing to groups like "welfare chiselers," elite intellectuals, environmental and consumer activists, and government bureaucrats as the source of frustrated opportunity and failed dreams. For over a decade, citizen organizing had expressed such discontent in different terms, through ongoing organizations that mobilized people to seek power for themselves, their neighbors, and other similarly powerless groups.

But the very sense of powerlessness toward large scale institutions that citizen groups addressed and the seriousness of their intention to empower ordinary people also had led to a widespread skepticism about any involvement in "politics as usual."

Carolyn Lucas was raising two small children when a neighbor invited her to attend a meeting about large corporations that were delinquent in their property taxes. She was far from an "activist." "During the Vietnam War," recalls Lucas, who had grown up in Boston, "I thought the protesters were crazy. I was very conservative." But she was outraged to find that large businesses in Boston owed many millions of dollars in back property taxes—the main source of city revenues—and the city was doing little about it.[5]

Massachusetts Fair Share was the organization working on the tax issue, and Lucas was surprised to see that ordinary people were making plans and developing a strategy for how to deal with it. "It was wonderful. Here, the people doing the talking were not some educated somebody but people like myself." She found the meetings a fascinating opportunity to learn the real dynamics of local government, taxes, and who pays the bills. "There was all this knowledge out there that you never saw in the newspapers, and had never learned about in school. We found out piece by piece." When Fair Share called a large meeting with city officials to talk about one restaurant that owed fifty thousand dollars in back taxes, "I found I had a speaking role, challenging the assistant assessor of the City of Boston. I was shaking like a leaf." But Lucas was also more knowledgeable than the officials. The organization soon succeeded, forcing not only the payment of taxes owed but also ten thousand dollars in interest.

Lucas quickly became an eloquent and effective leader of the state organization. The very concerns that had led her to involvement in Fair Share, however, led her to make a strict separation between citizen groups and election campaigns. "I joined Fair Share because it was apart from elections," she remembered. "Ordinary people found institutions are simply not responsive and we need something else. My father was a member of his union for thirty years, and then he tore up his union card because he was so angry. It had gotten so out of touch."

Massachusetts Fair Share's organizing experiences also led, however, to a growing realization that simply avoiding elections was like "fighting with one hand behind our back," as Lucas put it. Over time, the arsenal of tactics—holding meetings to pressure elected officials, holding demonstrations or public events intended to spotlight wrongdoing, and the like—"lost some of the element of surprise," according to Miles Rapoport. Rapoport, who had been on the staff of Massachusetts Fair Share and later directed the Connecticut Citizen Action Group, described how by the late 1970s more and more leaders and organizers had come to feel that "we could do much better on the issues we cared about if ultimately we had the power to say to politicians, 'Next time we're going to work to unseat you.'" In other terms, political leaders who regularly supported citizen group initiatives began to ask what positive help they might get for their efforts. During a 1978 campaign in Massachusetts for property tax relief for low and moderate income citizens, Lucas found that Fair Share's access to leading state politicians was less than that of groups that could turn out for smaller numbers of people for meetings or events. "What did the other groups do that we didn't?" Lucas wondered. The answer was clear enough. "They worked to elect candidates."[6]

Meanwhile, other groups in the emerging networks of citizen organizations had pioneered electoral involvement, with considerable effectiveness. In California, the Campaign for Economic Democracy, or CED, that grew out of Tom Hayden's race for the U.S. Senate in 1976 won a number of election campaigns and, in cities like Santa Monica, helped progressive populist tickets come to power. Indeed, Hayden and others had founded the CED out of the conviction that American politics would increasingly be shaped "by a conflict between right wing populism and a progressive populist movement that is from the bottom up, founded in local and state efforts," as he described it. Almost from the beginning the Ohio Public Interest Campaign saw electoral races as an important part of a broad strategy.

In 1977 in Cleveland, a spontaneous public outcry from neighborhood groups and others in the city arose over a series of give-aways by city government to large business and banking interests. First, the popular city-owned utility, Municipal Light, was offered for sale. Then in two summer months, June and July, the city council sought to give three large tax breaks or "abatements" to business interests, National City Bank, Stouffer's Corporation, and Sohio Oil. "In a small period, an unprecedented public sentiment was unleashed," remembered Jay Westbrook, at that time staff director for OPIC in the city. "There were crowds of people all the time marching through City Hall, testifying, protesting." The city response made citizens even angrier. A meeting of city council scheduled to make a final decision on the National City Bank abatement failed to convene at 8 P.M., while hundreds of people waited in the public gallery. Finally, someone discovered the council was meeting in a secret session in a locked room across the hall. "the crowd streamed out and started chanting, "We want the council, we want the council.""

The tax abatements were widely perceived as simply a boondoggle. In a five-part series, the local newspaper studied where tax abatements had been tried and concluded it made little difference to whether companies stayed or left an area. In the case of the bank, chartered for Ohio, the arguments about job loss or relocation seemed transparently ridiculous to many citizens. Fired by the issue, a number of candidates challenged incumbents, and OPIC found itself in the key role of city-wide mobilizer, pulling together a city-wide coalition of neighborhood organizations, churches, unions, senior citizens, and others. "You Can't Run Cleveland if You Sell It Out," headlined the leaflet prepared for challengers. "Ask the Candidate: Whose Voice Will You Listen To?" In the election, almost one third of the old council, ten members, lost their seats in what the *Plain Dealer* called "The Tuesday Night Massacre." The *Cleveland Call and Post* headlined, "City Council Gets a Facelift as Voters Revolt on Muny Light and Tax Abatement."[7]

Two years later, Jay Westbrook won a city council seat himself, again against an incumbent, and soon became the visible center of opposition to the Republican mayor, George Voinovich. By the time Citizen Action formed as a national organization, OPIC had considerable experience in elections. "We knew how to integrate electoral politics into the life of a citizen organization," explained Ira Arlook. "We were an organization that also did electoral politics. Electoral politics was one part of an overall strategy." The canvass, in particular, proved an immense aid in electoral action. During a crucial city council race in Cincinnati in 1981, Tom Brush, the incumbent champion of OPIC's "right-to-know" about toxics legislation seemed certain to be defeated by a conservative effort to unseat him that was lavishly funded by the Republican Party and supported by business groups like Proctor and Gamble and the Chamber of Commerce. An intensive effort by the canvass in the last twelve weeks of the election, combining extensive voter identification, a phone bank, and follow-up mailings, changed the complexion of the race. Whereas in the previous election Brush had won thirty-six thousand votes and finished ninth, just barely making it into the council, in 1981 his total increased to 49,500 with the same voter turnout, just five hundred votes behind the all-time largest spender for Cincinnati elections. The right-to-know bill, which had seemed dead before the election, was passed in seven months. Two years later, Marian Spencer, a steering committee member of OPIC in Cincinnati, was elected. Spencer's victory to city council was the first in the city's history for a black woman, the first nonincumbent to win a seat since since 1975.[8]

The election of Ronald Reagan to the White House in 1980 rapidly accelerated the interest of citizen groups in electoral action. On the one hand, it symbolized a shift taking place across the country that made the very terms of citizen organizing more difficult: pressuring elected officials to respond to corporate abuses only worked if they were not intransigently pro big business. Ideologues for large corporations, such as those most often elected by new right wing campaigns, were far more difficult to deal with. On the other hand, citizen leaders looked at the political successes of the right wing and contrasted them to the organizing track record of progressive citizen groups, which, as *New York Times* national reporter John Herbers observed, was often greater in actual mobilization of ordinary Americans. As Heather Booth put it, "These groups on the right have no greater ability to organize or deal with the issues than progressive citizen organizations. In fact, their promise of actually empowering citizens is a completely hollow one. But they've been winning significant power at every level because they paid attention to elections."

Immediately following the election, the new Citizen Action group held a Leadership Conference in Cleveland and concluded that "we must bring the power of our organizations into the electoral arena" in order to respond to the anticipated attack on communities. By 1982, they began training groups in the nuts and bolts of elections. In its first year, they assisted citizen groups working in 122 local, state, and congressional campaigns, winning 70 percent of the races in which they were involved. "This organization soon proved one of the most sophisticated political operations in the country," observed Paul Tully, a veteran political consultant.[9]

Citizen groups began to think about how to translate the skills of grass roots organizing into political terms. As a part of that process, in turn, they often experienced pressure to give much more explicit attention to what they believed in. "It became increasingly clear that the debate in the whole country was not simply about issues but about questions of value and a vision of the future," explained Michael Ansara, founding director of Massachusetts Fair Share. "There was the need to shift from the strongly pragmatic, issue focus of organizing in the early seventies to the development of a language that could tap the values and vision of people to step out of their daily lives." Such a process was important, in part, for organizational sustenance. "We needed to look at the longer term program that could sustain what we did over time." And it was also a vital dimension of electoral involvement. "In politics, you have to respond to a much wider range of concerns than in issue organizing, where you pick the issues to address. We needed an organizational culture that was much more value based." In-depth interviews and discussions with leaders across the state led to the Fair Share Program of 1982. Declaring that "we believe that major change is absolutely necessary," the document continued that members "do not want change merely for its own sake. We are for changes that flow from deeply held, traditional values [now] being violated by many of the current policies of decision-makers in both government and business." The program listed ten basic principles:

> Democracy. We reaffirm our belief in the democratic principles upon which this country was founded. Democracy requires people to be organized, to be educated, to be empowered. We must extend democracy into the economic system so that decisions can reflect the interests and participation of employees, communities, consumers and the nation as a whole. As technology changes our society, we need to develop forms that can extend democracy so that we are not forced to deify experts and sacrifice our democratic rights to technocracy.

> The Family. The family, in all its varied forms, must be the primary unit of society. It must be cherished and supported and given an environment in which it can thrive. We support an individual's right to choose a personal lifestyle and family structure. Our current culture makes it harder and harder to nourish the values of family life in all its variety. All economic and governmental policy must be examined through the prism of support for the family.

> Quality of Life. Our country's vast resources must be used so that an improving quality of life is the rule for all our people, not the exception. The quality of our lives cannot be measured simply by the size of our paychecks or the GNP. It also has to do with the quality of our personal and family relationships, the food we eat, and the products we buy. We cannot go on wasting and consuming so much of the world's resources with reckless abandon. We need

to elevate the importance of quality over quantity: of products, of education, of the environment. We must develop new criteria which embrace these goals and reject economic growth which brings about a decline in quality, more but less meaningful jobs, and resources channeled only to a few. We can have economic growth which actually produces a rising standard and quality of living in the fullest sense.

Work. We believe in *meaningful work* as the key ingredient for personal fulfillment. We are becoming a society that devalues work and says instead that you are what you consume, what you buy, what you own. We believe in an ethic which values, respects and fairly rewards hard work. We believe in the right of all employees to organize associations and unions in freedom and security.

Neighborhoods and Community. We believe strongly in the importance of our neighborhoods. They are the lifeblood of our cities and towns. Strengthening, stabilizing and enriching them is part of a larger effort to meet the basic need of all people for a sense of strong and cooperative community.

Fairness and Equality. We believe in simple values of fairness and equality. What is good for one should be good for all. We are willing to make sacrifices for the common good, but not if we alone are sacrificing.

Respect and Tolerance. We believe that our society and values must be deeply imbued with respect: for all humans and human life; for the environment over which we have stewardship, not domination; for the wisdom and integrity of our elders; for all regardless of race, religion, or gender; for the needs of children; for the rights of others; for the ideas of minorities; for the needs of the majority; for other nations, other cultures and the self-determination of all nations.

Security. We believe that society should value security. *Personal Security*, to free us from random violence, crime, rape, unemployment, disabling injury or illness. *Community Security*, to free our neighborhoods from destruction because of highways or airports, deteriorating housing and absentee slumlords, hazardous wastes and toxic materials. *Economic Security*—for our families, communities, and nation. *National Security*, based on being part of a world at peace, working at decent and democratic relationships with other countries.

Initiative and Self-Reliance. The growth and sheer power of unaccountable corporate and government bureaucracies threatens the self-reliance of our people. Meaningful rewards for initiative and self-reliance go hand in hand with democracy, decentralization and remotivating our people. An activist government is a positive response to a society that needs changes. But at every point government should seek to empower citizens, communities and voluntary associations and should seek to stimulate a spirit of self-reliance based upon respect, work, equality, cooperation and democracy.

Organization. The final value we cherish is the value of grassroots democratic organization. Organization empowers, and provides a way to elevate values and act on them. Organization makes democracy real; it educates and changes people. Organization based on all the above values is essential in realizing those values.[10]

As citizen groups like Fair Share began to make explicit their underlying principles, the language of populism and the populist tradition began to win a widening currency as the overarching philosophy that tied such values together.

The populist political tradition had never really disappeared. Harry Truman had drawn on the legacy when he asked during his whistle stop tour during the 1948 election, "Are the special privilege boys going to run the country or are the people going to run it?" And populism was in the tradition of Martin Luther King Jr. as he looked to the democratic American alternative to racial bigotry and unbridled, unresponsive power. Indeed, King often made the populist point that racial prejudice was a tool of the power structure. Its "ghastly results," he argued, "have not been borne alone by the Negro. Poor white men, women and children, bearing the scars of ignorance, deprivation and poverty, are evidence of the fact that harm to one is injury to all."[11]

In the 1960s, Robert Kennedy was the most prominent progressive candidate arguing a populist message in the Democratic Party. His presidential campaign in 1968 suggested the potency of populist appeals, by drawing support from black constituencies as well as the urban ethnic and rural populations that had previously supported George Wallace. In 1972, two former Kennedy staff members, Jeff Greenfield and Jack Newfield, published a book, *A Populist Manifesto: The Making of a New Majority*, that argued, simply, "Some institutions and people have too much money and power, most people have too little, and the first priority of politics must be to redress that imbalance." Then in 1976, Fred Harris, senator from Oklahoma, entered the Democratic Party primaries on a "new populist" program. Though Harris failed to win the nomination, he succeeded in reintroducing the term and spirit into the political mainstream. Indeed, Jimmy Carter periodically referred to himself as a populist that year. And his campaign staff brought together a number of people—Jim Hightower, Lane Evans, Barbara Shailor, Jim Rosapepe, and others—who would later play important roles in the evolution of the movement.[12]

Jim Hightower, especially, became a nationally visible embodiment of populism. In 1982, Hightower, former editor of the *Texas Observer* and author of two books on agricultural issues, ran for commissioner of agriculture in Texas. When Hightower declared his candidacy, the incumbent, Reagan Brown, quipped, "I've never even heard of Jim Hightower. I'm gonna beat him like a drum." As the race heated up, Brown said the Viet Cong had infiltrated Hightower's campaign staff. "We beat the Medfly, and we're gonna beat the gadfly."[13]

Hightower, a slender man dressed in a big white western hat and cowboy boots, proved fiesty, quickwitted, and legendary for his comebacks. He replied that Brown's tenure in office had done little or nothing to help thousands of struggling family farmers. "There is a lot more to being agriculture commissioner than putting a straw in your mouth and humming, 'Thank God, I'm a country boy,'" said Hightower, urging someone to read the man his books so he would know something about agriculture. "Brown's record is as ugly as my face." Putting together what he called a populist alliance of farmers, community organizations like Communities Organized for Public Service (COPS) in San Antonio, trade unions, and others, Hightower went on to win nearly 60 percent of the primary vote and beat his Republican opponent, who sought to get headlines with his charge that Hightower was unmarried and lacked a refrigerator.[14]

Once Hightower was in office, his innovative farm policies soon earned him national attention. He helped watermelon farmers form cooperatives, aided the Texas wine industry, worked to revive farmers markets in urban areas around the state, and sought to create new pools of capital for aid to cooperative food processing. "In 10 years, the farmer's share of the food dollar has fallen from 37 cents to 28 cents and it's going lower," he explained. "The money's in processing." Through his work as chair of the Democratic National Committee's Agricultural Council, he did much to shape the party's position on farm policies. His ideas on an alternative to the administration approach came directly from farmers and activist rural groups across the country, expressed through a series of hearings that the leaders of the new Populist Caucus had sponsored. The Caucus, in turn, was partly the brainchild of Tom Harkin, the congressman from Iowa who successfully challenged the conservative incumbent senator, Roger Jepsen, in the 1984 election, becoming one of the striking exceptions to the Reagan landslide of that year.[15]

Tom Harkins's father was a coal miner and farmer in Iowa, a strong advocate of unions but also a fan of the demogogic "populist" Father Coughlin during the Depression. "For years, I thought populists were racist, red-necks, know nothings," Harkin recounted. In the 1960s, Harkin served in the Navy, and what he saw turned him strongly against the Vietnam War.[16]

As a congressional aide, he went back to Vietnam in the summer of 1970 as part of a fact finding mission in the wake of the U.S. invasion of Cambodia. Frustrated by much of the congressional delegation's unwillingness to hear much more than military briefings, Harkin followed up leads on his own. He found a former prisoner on Con Son Island who confirmed rumors that the South Vietnamese tortured dissident student activists and Buddhist leaders and held them in small "tiger cages." Harkin's pictures of the cages, published in *Life* magazine, added to the American public outcry about the war and cost him his congressional job. Barred from staff, he decided to run for Congress himself. He came close in 1972. He won in 1974. In Congress, Harkin established a reputation as hardworking, knowledgeable, and effective on issues ranging from farm policy to science and technology. Then, in the aftermath of Republican sweeps of both Iowa Senate seats, he began to think about running against Jepsen.

Reading the *Populist Moment*, Lawrence Goodwyn's dramatic account of the first populist movement, deeply moved Harkin and led him to extensive reading in the field. "It was like the scales fell from my eyes," he said. In 1983 he signed up fourteen representatives as founders of a new Populist Caucus—Jim Weaver of Oregon (whose great-grandfather had been the Populist Party presidential candidate), Robert Wise of West Virginia (who had been an officer of West Virginia Citizen Action), Gerry Sikorski of Minnesota, Lane Evans of Illinois, Albert Gore of Tennessee, Byron Dorgan of North Dakota, and others.

Populist Caucus members drew direct inspiration from the first movement. "A reporter asked me when it formed 'how can Richard Viguerie, the right wing fundraiser, also call himself a populist?'," Harkin remembered. "I asked him to see if Viguerie would agree to run on the Populist Party platform of 1892. I certainly would. It had a lot of good ideas that just need updating." But they saw the needs well to update the tradition. "The term 'populist' has a touch of demagoguery associated with it from history," explained Paul Simon, the freshman senator from Illinois who brought eloquence and thoughtfulness to populism. "We need to stress its progressive dimension, and to point out that right wing populism is a wolf in sheep's clothing, that destroys the things it says it's for." Simon believes that progressive populism champions the idea of government responsive to the needs of the average citizen, and it also provides a kind of schooling. "A group like Citizen Action offers an alternative to this politics of greed, to the leaders who appeal to the selfish in us. It combines self-interest and humanitarianism. There's a little of the noble and the beast in everyone. Organizing and political leadership can bring out one or the other."

The Caucus's statement of principles compared the first Populists with the situation of ordinary citizens today. "One hundred years ago," it began, "the Populist Party, a movement of ordinary citizens, farmers, small businessmen, and laborers, formed in the West and the South. It was a movement to restore to government and society the principles of economic independence and equity. It was a movement to return economic power to the common citizen." [17]

"The Populists ultimately won many of their demands. Yet many of the injustices faced by the Populists continue today," it went on. "Monied interests still exert a disproportionate influence over the government. The voices of common citizens are still not adequately heard in Congress. Basic inequities still plague the political process." Calling for "a strong government that fights for the economic rights of all Americans, not a big, unjust government that lets wealthy and powerful elites strangle our economic freedoms," the statement advocated five initial principles:

Our government should protect the common citizen from the excessive power of special interest groups.
The burden of taxation should be distributed equally.
Congress should insure that money is available at reasonable rates of interest and must exercise more control over the Federal Reserve Board.
The excessive influence of corporations and other special interest groups on elections should be reduced.
Our natural resources should be preserved and protected from exploitation.[18]

In the ninety-eighth session of Congress, in 1983 and 1984, Populist Caucus members played a key role in the fight against deregulation of natural gas, in the effort to save family farms, and on several other issues. Most important perhaps, all members of the caucus won election, often by striking margins in states that Ronald Reagan carried overwhelmingly. In political terms, few things succeed like success. When the caucus reconvened in the ninety-ninth session, it included twenty-two members of the House of Representatives—with urban populist advocates like Barbara Mikulski, Charles Hayes, Marcy Kaptur, and Al Wheat—and three of the four freshmen Democratic senators—Tom

Harkin, Albert Gore, and Paul Simon. It soon established an information clearinghouse and resource center, the Populist Forum, headed by Jane Perkins, a former city council member from Harrisburg, Pennsylvania, who had worked closely with Penn PIC. And the new national group began to develop ties with local and state officials across the country. Their objectives were ambitious: "to promote the Populist philosophy and identify those who share those ideas at the state and local levels" and "to set the agenda for debate within the Democratic Party and our nation for the next decade."

The feasibility of such goals grew not simply from political networks but from the strong bases that had also begun to develop out of citizen organizing across the country. In authentic populist fashion, the political movement's long range strength was seen to rely heavily on such local bases as the training ground for future congressional candidates and the source of creative initiatives and ideas. "Our emphasis on the local level is still the best," explained Willie Velasquez, director of the Southwest Voter Registration Education Project, a voter registration effort that has worked closely with Hightower and community groups. In particular, the network of strong community organizations pioneered by Communities Organized for Public Service in San Antonio has given an extraordinary depth and power to local activism in a number of cities in Texas and elsewhere in the Southwest. "The great increase in registration among Hispanics has come from concentrating on those kinds of elections." Across the country in Connecticut, groundwork for populist politics had been laid before Connecticut Citizen Action Group began to participate directly in election campaigns by the Legislative Electoral Action Program, or LEAP, a coalition of progressive groups that had also challenged politics as usual as practiced by both Democratic and Republican parties.[19]

CCAG's first director, Toby Moffett, set a precedent for electoral action by running for Congress and winning in 1974. In 1980, Marc Caplan, the director of CCAG before Miles Rapoport moved down from Boston, brought together a number of labor union leaders to talk about rebuilding a progressive political presence in the state, long dominated by business oriented Democrats. "We had been involved in politics for many years," explained John Flynn, New England and New York political director of the United Automobile Workers and first president of LEAP. "We felt we had to reach out to other people beyond our traditional borders." One of the first recruits to the LEAP board was Ladislaus (Laddie) Michalowski, a long time activist in the labor movement, who had become a dynamic leader in CCAG as well and was determined to build bridges between community organizations and workers.[20]

Michalowski was born into a Polish immigrant family, part of the closeknit Polish neighborhood in New Britain, Connecticut. He grew up a staunch conservative, supporting Herbert Hoover, arguing the Republican point of view in high school. But his father's deadly disease, silicosis, contracted by breathing silicon dust at the brass factory where he worked as a molder, and his experiences of the Great Depression changed his ideas. "I had always supported the underdog," he explained, "even as a conservative. When I began to work in the shop, I saw the low wages and the conditions, and each week we worked less and less." When workers in the brass factory—the same his father had once worked in—heard about union organizing, they contacted the organizer and asked for help. "He gave us a meeting date in two weeks and it spread like wildfire. You can't picture what organizing was like then. By the next meeting we had two hundred people. In several months, we had several thousand who had joined the union."[21]

Michalowski remained active in community and political affairs, even after persecution during the McCarthy era of the 1950s had driven out the union and cost him his job. In the sixties, he proudly supported his daughter, a college student, who had gone south to work in civil rights, and he raised money for blacks seeking to register in Mississippi. Then when CCAG appeared on the scene, Michalowski saw it as an exciting revival of the sort of activity that had initially inspired him. "I have a basic theory that the success in bringing about any advance for people is going to be based on the number of people that get involved," he explained. "CCAG gets more people into action around things they're fighting for than I have seen since the New Deal days." He also participated in LEAP. And when CCAG began to consider electoral involvement, Michalowski became chair of its Political Action Committee and made it a part of LEAP. He saw the new coalition as a unique opportunity for labor unions to revive. "Labor has suffered greatly in recent years because of the splits they went through. They've been on the defensive. So a coalition with community groups is good for labor." It was also good, in his view, for the community. "Labor has resources. Community groups will never be able to win anything significant without that coalition." In 1982, Doreen Del Bianco, CCAG co-chair, won election to the state legislature in a remarkable upset against the well-established incumbent, with considerable help from LEAP and CCAG members. In 1984, Miles Rapoport, CCAG director, ran and won against Joan Kemler, one of the major powers in the state Democratic Party. As a result of such campaigns, labor became convinced of the need for such new alliances. "It's now officially recognized that this is important," Michalowski explained. "My old bones shake when I realize how it's turned around in the last couple of years."

Activist legislators like Del Bianco and Rapoport have seen their elections as creating a new sort of political leadership, closely tied to the citizen movement. "The CCAG lobbyist and I spent a lot of time together developing strategy for CCAG issues," Del Bianco described. When the organization brought citizens from around the state to the capitol for a "Lobby Day" to talk about its key issues, Del Bianco addressed the group. "I loved it. The legislature can be so stuffy. But Lobby Day was like fresh air. Here were hundreds of normal people walking around the halls with signs, and legislators squirming." With the combination of CCAG lobbying power, Del Bianco, and a few other legislators, several key issues made rapid progress. The group was able to get passed the first bill in the country putting a cap on the costs of a nuclear power plant and the first bill prohibiting the landfill of hazardous waste.[22]

Other citizen groups were also finding success in building coalitions combining issues and politics. Montcel in Montana and CAPA and Fair Share in Idaho translated this out west. And it began to take off around the country. Ron Charity, manager of numerous campaigns in Virginia, said, "My twenty years' experience convinces me that combining the political process and grass roots organizations is essential for creating a more responsible democracy. It's especially important in the South, where citizen action has such potential."

Nineteen eighty-three was a year of major black political successes. In Chicago, Harold Washington won over the Democratic establishment and his Republican opponent. In Charlotte, North Carolina, neighborhood organizations, women's groups, environmentalists and others joined to elect Harvey Gantt. This victory furthered the growth of the Carolina Community Project, a multi-issue citizens' organization. "It was a black white coalition in the deep South, where many people said it couldn't happen," described Si Kahn, who lived there. "Different groups came together about the question, what kind of city are we going to have and who is going to run it, the developers or the citizens?" In Philadelphia, Wilson Goode beat Frank Rizzo. Through all these and other campaigns, large numbers of new minority voters were registered.

Penn PIC's door to door canvass operation knocked on more than twenty-eight thousand doors and followed up with mailings, phone banks, volunteer house meetings, and a public hearing. Moreover, in areas of Philadelphia like the sprawling west side, a new generation of young black leadership emerged that was to play a key role in the organization's development.[23]

Vince Hughes had grown up in West Philadelphia, in an all-black lower middle class community. "Good, solid people who wanted their kids to get through school and do the right thing," as he described it. But spreading poverty undermined large areas of the west side. In some communities, infant mortality rates by the 1980s had begun to reach levels of Third World nations and rates of cancer were the worst in the state. Families were ravaged by unemployment and teenage pregnancies.

In 1982, Hughes, an active leader of the AFSCME union district in town and vice chair of its political arm, PEOPLE, had helped with the successful political campaign for the state legislature of Chaka Fattah. Fattah was the son of community leader Sister Falaka and David Fattah, whose House of Umoja for young teenagers had helped stem a devastating wave of gang violence and had become a national symbol of community self-help and revitalization. Out of the campaign came an ongoing organization that then went to work in the Goode election of

1983. "Neighborhood people were the cutting edge of the Wilson Goode movement," Hughes remembered. "And a lot of them were young, my age, twenty-five, twenty-six, twenty-seven. Goode made them feel participants." In 1984, Hughes himself took on the well entrenched incumbent in the district adjoining Fattah's. Waging an aggressive grass roots campaign that knocked on more than fifty thousand doors, he came close to victory, and prepared the way for future races.

Such political activities on the west side meshed with Penn PIC's electoral work and grass roots organizing around issues like health care. Hughes became a leader in Penn PIC because, like his political campaign, "it has the philosophy that you have to take the issue to the people." In Hughes's view, populism means issues like toxic waste, health care, housing, grass roots economic development. But it means, equally, a different style of politics and leadership that simultaneously challenges people, organizes people, and listens to people. "It's what I call transformational leadership," Hughes explained. In his view, "Too much of the Democratic Party is transactional leadership, just buying into the system." [24]

Alma Hill, a warm, dynamic woman of deep religious conviction, has practiced transformational leadership since coming to Trenton, New Jersey, in 1956. Hill had been born in South Carolina. She remembers the horror of the night in 1936 when her brother, injured in an automobile wreck, was unable to go to the hospital because he was black. "He was in a lot of pain. He screamed the entire night." His suffering and death fueled her determination to be a nurse and help other people.

Hill was trained in New York City and then worked at Metropolitan Hospital after World War II, supervising research work in geriatrics. "Nursing taught us to organize, to be able to deal with crises, to switch horses in midstream. I developed an attitude that nothing is made in concrete." When she and her family moved to Trenton, she put her skills and attitude to work in a wide range of community affairs, from programs for unwed teenage mothers to neighborhood revitalization. Hill also became a mainstay of her church. She chaired the Ecumenical Movement Organization in Trenton. She became a leading figure of Church Women United on state and national levels. In 1982, the New Jersey Council of

Churches honored her as "Christian of the Year" in a state-wide ceremony, with family and friends coming in from across the country.

When New Jersey Citizen Action began, Art Jones, the second black president of the state Council of Churches in its history, suggested that Hill was essential to involve. "Jeanne Marie Oterson, the organizer, sat down to talk about church involvement," Hill remembers. "I was excited because the organization was including the church from the beginning. Too many bring the church in after everything is planned and formulated." Hill became co-chair of New Jersey Citizen Action and helped lead campaigns on issues ranging from plant closings to toxic waste. In 1984, the organization undertook a major nonpartisan voter registration campaign, signing up tens of thousands of new voters. "It brought together groups for the first time that knew no ethnic bounds," said Hill. "We organized locally, and got volunteers and money from the churches and other groups. We built trust between different groups that had never worked together before—people against more nuclear weapons and the farmers, people working on schools. Our policy was that if you worked together with us on voter registration, we will engage the issues you are interested in in the future.[25]

In Ohio, OPIC undertook large voter registration drives in many cities. In September, 1984, voter registration director Gloria Fauss visited a food stamp office in Cincinnati as part of a frequent strategy to sign people up to vote in waiting rooms, where the poor often had to sit for several hours before their names were called.[26]

"I had been talking to people about an hour," Fauss remembered, "when suddenly a security guard asked what I was doing. I explained, and showed him a copy of the court order we had about our right to register people to vote." The man was not impressed. He called in squad cars from around the city, and, eventually, the chief of police, all of whom demanded that Fauss leave. When Fauss refused, pointing out politely that she was a registrar and simply exercising her constitutional rights, the police handcuffed her, took her to jail, subjected her to a strip search, and kept her overnight.

Newspapers across the state headlined the story the next day: "Police Strip Search Vote Registrar"; "Sign Up of Voters Risky Job"; "Registrar's Arrest Sparks an Uproar"; "Vote Registrar Arrest Called Outrage." It fueled an enormous movement to the polls. "All sorts of people came up and said, 'I wasn't really going to vote but after what they did to that woman I will,'" Fauss recounted. "Volunteers came out of the woodwork." The total they registered in 1984 working with other groups (Citizens' Leadership Foundation and Project Vote) amounted to over a hundred thousand in the state. Carol Browner, with the Citizen Leadership Foundation, stressed the long term impact of these voter registration drives. "By joining issue campaigns and voter registration, these new registrants will be more likely to understand the alternatives and their stake in it and, therefore, be more likely to vote and become active citizens."[27]

Voter registration has long been a priority in civil rights movements in American history. In the Deep South, registration programs of the NAACP, the Southern Christian Leadership Conference, the Student Nonviolent Coordinating Committee, the Voter Education Project, and others had been at the heart of civil rights. Subsequent efforts like the National Coalition for Black Voter Participation and the Southwest Voter Registration Project had a dramatic impact on the political balance in many areas. Then, in the early 1980s, activists in black, Mexican, and other communities had come to see voter registration as a key issue of empowerment. Jesse Jackson's remarkable success in mobilizing and inspiring millions of voters in 1984 added to the momentum of the effort. By the mid-eighties, voter registration groups proliferated in a wide range of arenas: ACORN, the Churches Committee on Voter Registration/ Education, Citizens Leadership Foundation (founded by Heather Booth), Citizenship Education Fund, Humanserve, League of Women Voters Education Fund, Midwest Voter Registration/Education Project, Operation Big Vote, Project Vote, Public Interest Research Group, the Women's Vote Project, and others. All had as their core principle the conviction that voting should be seen—as it is seen in virtually every other major industrial society—as a natural and intrinsic part of what it means to be a citizen. One registers at birth, at marriage, for the draft, and for work, but why not automatically when one reaches eighteen register to vote as well? Foundations interested in grass roots citizen empowerment and the inclusion of those left out of the system have been essential to such work.

New effective alliances have developed through this work in the electoral arena. In New York, the Citizen Action affiliate built strong community chapters in several areas of the state through work on issues such as toxic waste and utility rate increases. Meanwhile, union leaders like Jan Pierce, vice president of the Communications Workers of America, had long championed labor involvement in civic affairs and had played a key role in previous political upsets, like Mario Cuomo's gubernatorial race. In 1984, Pierce and leaders of seven other major unions, (including the United Automobile Workers, the Service Employees International Union, the Food and Commercial Workers, the American Federation of Teachers, and the American Federation of State, County and Municipal Employees), joined together to create a coalition. Working on a state level and in many local areas as well, the coalition brought together unions with neighborhood organizations, senior citizen associations, and environmental, women's, tenant, and peace groups for voter registration and voter education. After the elections, all these groups created the new, much larger Citizen Action of New York. It will undertake electoral campaigns and organizing efforts alike, around issues that range from toxic waste and housing to economic development.[28]

Thus, a blend of organizing and electoral action had begun to achieve a growing visibility by the mid-eighties. In the midst of the Reagan administration's second term, it was still a political force in its infancy. And the ways it would eventually evolve were impossible to predict. But already the key feature of populist politics was evident, voiced, in different ways, by leading populist political figures and citizen leaders alike.

As in the first Populist movement, authentic populist politics today aims at genuine citizen empowerment, the development of the skills, resources, knowledge, and organizational tools necessary for ordinary people to gain a real voice in decision making. Tom Harkin makes the point by describing the difference between "public opinion" and "public will."[29]

In Harkin's view, "Public opinion is a knee jerk reaction, an instant response to something that doesn't sound right. Public will is something deeper. It has to do with people's understanding, their deepest motivations, what they feel is important for themselves and their community and their society." The process of organizing and political action "should point to that. It gives people the information and data that they don't get from the utilities or the bureaucracies which they need to make an informed decision. Ultimately, populism gives people hope, a way to change things."[30]

According to Chuck Deppert, a co-chair of Citizen Action, citizen organizing is a far richer understanding of politics than simply electing people to office. "I've been involved in a lot of elections, and I know they're necessary. But you can get yourself so involved in a campaign that you get tied to a candidate. Then if he goes down the tubes, so does your credibility. We have to have independent citizen groups that give people a voice on an ongoing basis."[31]

In its development, populism in the 1980s and 1990s has a rich legacy to draw upon for inspiration and lessons alike. But it also suggests the beginnings of an alternative vision for America's future, that would take the ideals of the past and reframe them in ways relevant to the world we are entering.

9. DEMOCRATIC VISIONS

If there is no struggle, there is no progress. Those who profess to favor freedom yet deprecate agitation are men who want crops without plowing up the ground. They want rain without thunder and lightning. They want the ocean without the awful roar of its many waters. . . . Power concedes nothing without demand. It never did and never will.

Frederick Douglass, abolitionist

Ours is a grand and holy mission . . . to drive from our land and forever abolish the triune monopoly of land, [of money], and transportation. We need to raise less corn and more hell.

Mary Lease, Populist leader, 1892

Citizen Organizing: Religious and Moral Roots

The Book of Isaiah in the Bible says that people without a vision shall perish," says Cora Tucker. "There's been a deception going on about what the American dream is. It's not what we've been hearing—where the Big Fish eat up the little ones. We have to take back the American dream from the New Right and redefine what it is." The Book of Isaiah also saw a true people's vision emerging only as they "build up the ancient ruins" and "repair the devastations of many generations." [1]

The moral foundation of progressive populism and of citizen organizations places them in sharp conflict with the dominant interests in our society, as the preceding chapters have shown. The tradition of citizen activism is one that balances self-interest with concern for others, one's career with the life of one's community, one's group with a broader, more pluralist appreciation for the great diversity of peoples and heritages in our land.

Such an understanding also animates our mainstream religious traditions. For the Puritans, God's covenant meant a community. 'We must delight in each other," said John Winthrop in 1633, "make others' conditions our own, rejoice together, mourn together and suffer together, always having before our eyes our commission and community in the work." The notion of community, in Jewish, Catholic, and Protestant thought, necessarily entails a commitment to justice as well. "Thus says the Lord," reads the Book of Jeremiah, "do justice and righteousness and deliver from the hand of the oppressor him who has been robbed." In the Book of Leviticus, God describes the year of Jubilee as coming every fifty years, during which people are "to proclaim liberty to the inhabitants" and return all lands to the common pool to prevent great concentrations of wealth and power. When Jesus spoke of his mission, he declared his intention to bring such a year, "the Year of the Lord." [2]

Such values have been the wellspring for almost every broad democratic movement in American history, and they infuse democratic populism today as well. "People who become involved in Oregon Fair Share become involved in the community," explained Lynn Cardiff. "They say, 'let's make this a better place to live, let's get jobs for our community, let's make the state better.'" For Alma Hill, the gospel makes specific demands and provides deep resources. "The idea of doing unto others as I would have them do unto me—nobody said it's going to be easy," she explained. "But by practicing faith, you're on the right track. If you know God is there when you are in need, you don't worry about tomorrow. We concentrate on what we need to do today." [3]

These rich traditions of involvement, justice, community, and individual dignity have found expression in the vision of America as a land of many peoples, not just a single "people." In the 1850s, Herman Melville, returning from Europe, sailed past the Statue of Liberty and wrote that "we are heirs of all time, and with all nations we divide our inheritance. On this great continent all tribes and peoples of the world are forming into one great federated whole." In citizen groups today, one finds the same insight. "I like living in this neighborhood because of the differences," explained Tom Moogan, leader of an interracial fight in a working class section of Brooklyn for more mortgage money that had been initiated by the New York Public Interest Research Group. Moogan recounted how the effort had taught the community residents, black and white, a new respect. "We have learned to explore our differences, and listen, and share them."[4]

In America today we remember too little about earlier traditions of protest and democratic change. Without a knowledge of their own history, people are disarmed in present struggles. If you don't know that many of the rights and comforts of life that you take for granted today were actually won in conflict, not given as a reward for complacency, how can you believe that you can have power and win now? If you don't know of the battles that led to the working day being eight hours instead of fourteen, or the struggle for public education, or for the right to vote for women, how can you envision changing seemingly overwhelming problems you face today? Only the mobilization and organization of the creative talents and energy of ordinary people can transform the problems we face into opportunities and possibilities. For those who enjoy wealth and power, the widespread myths of the powerlessness of the people are all too useful. If people think that nothing can be done to challenge seriously the shape of decision making, no one will try. Notions like "the free hand of the marketplace" and the "inevitability of economic dislocation" simply reinforce the sense that people, together, can do little about the great forces reshaping society. Only those who possess special expertise and knowledge can even begin to understand the shape of the future that is coming.

Elite and right wing domination of the terms of discussion about our nation's history, values, and goals is scarcely new. Ordinary people have regularly been told that "we come from nowhere and have no history." As Alice Palmer, director of the Black Press Institute and former member of the Citizen Action staff, put it, "Every major challenge to vested interests and unresponsive power has had to overcome the perception that the challengers have no integrity."

To understand where we are going—and can go—it is important to understand where we have come from. The clashes of values and principles today have old roots. Indeed, we are now in a new stage of a great conflict that reaches back as early as the first settlers from Europe.[5]

History: Struggles for American Democracy

In 1641, the Confederation of Portsmouth astonished the world with its constitution: "The government which this body politic doth attend unto . . . is a Democratic or Popular government." When America's founding fathers and mothers considered what forms of government to establish for the new nation, they modeled the Articles of Confederation, in part, on even older traditions of self-government long practiced by the native Iroquois Confederacy. According to Mercy Warren, one of America's great foremothers, "Government is instituted for the protection, safety and happiness of the people, and not for the profit, honor or private interest of any man, family or class of men." George Warner, a sailmaker in New York who helped lead a popular democratic movement in the early years of the republic, believed that "the means for the preservation of public liberty are tradesmen, mechanics and the industrious classes of society." In his view, "Wherever the influence of riches are able to direct the choice of public officers, there the downfall of liberty cannot be very far remote."[6]

Progressive populism stands directly in these democratic traditions. But there has always been a group of those who saw government, properly, as the handmaiden of great wealth. Alexander Hamilton, the nation's first Treasury Secretary, believed that "all communities divide themselves into the few and the many. The first are rich and well-born, the other the mass of the people." He had no doubt who should rule. "The people are turbulent and changing; they seldom judge or determine right. Give, therefore, to the first class a distinct, permanent share in government." Hamilton advocated the tremendous expansion of American material wealth as the arrangement most appropriate for "sorting out" those most fit to lead. And he believed in a vast military force, necessary to safeguard and advance American industrial interests. There should be, in his vision, "one great American system, superior to the control of all transatlantic forces or influence and able to dictate the terms of connection between the Old and the New World."[7]

For one candid industrialist in the late nineteenth century, Hamilton's words seemed simply self-evident truth. "We are not politicians or public thinkers," he said. "We are the rich. We own America. We got it, God knows how, but we intend to keep it." Today, leaders of big business similarly glory in their domination. "With top corporate leaders now out in front," wrote *Fortune* magazine, "business seems to possess all the primary instruments of power."[8]

But Hamilton's dream was not the nation's. States like Virginia, Kentucky, Pennsylvania, and Massachusetts called themselves "commonwealths" in their constitutions. More generally, the democratic wing of the American Revolution all thought of the nation as a commonwealth, bound together by a concern for the common good. The vision of the commonwealth had great power for our ancestors. In English history "commonwealth" had meant rule by the common people. But it had many other meanings as well. Commonwealth expressed the experiences of "the commons" in European countries, those grazing lands held jointly by the people. It drew on Biblical themes like the year of Jubilee. It was the "way things were" for the native Indians, before European settlement.

It is not surprising that the commonwealth was the enduring dream and language for American democratic movements. This was the vision of the first Populists as an alternative to a nation dominated by monopoly. It was the animating language of trade union movements. The commonwealth was memorialized in Joe Hill's song, "The Commonwealth of Toil." It was the program of midwestern movements like the Minnesota Farmer-Labor Party, the name of southern labor institutions like Commonwealth College, the guiding vision of the Washington Commonwealth Federation, which held a majority of seats in the state legislature in the 1940s. This dream surfaces today again.

Thus, in their *Pastoral Letter on Catholic Social Teaching and the U.S. Economy*, the Catholic bishops argue that a vision of economic justice cannot ignore certain basic questions:

Does our economic system place more emphasis on maximizing of profits than on meeting human needs and the fostering of human dignity?
Does our economy distribute its benefits equitably, or does it tend to concentrate power and resources in the hands of a few?
Does it promote excessive materialism and individualism?
Does it direct too many scarce resources to military purposes?
Does it adequately protect the environment and the nation's natural resources?

Such questions are more than a matter of simple "rights," the bishops argue. They involve recognizing what Martin Luther King Jr. called our moral interdependence. "Everyone has obligations based simply on membership in the social community," says the *Pastoral Letter*. "By fulfilling these duties, we create a true commonwealth."[9]

The fight today for economic justice is also the fight our ancestors waged. Again and again in American history the people have had to organize against large business interests. Mary Lease spoke for the first Populists, whose "grand and glorious crusade" had to battle those like the industrialist who claimed he "owned America." They fought, with considerable success, on behalf of an older vision. As the preface of the Populist Party of 1892 declared:

Corruption dominates the ballot box, the legislatures, the Congress and touches even the ermine of the bench. Assembled on the anniversary of the birth of the illustrious general who led the first great revolution on this continent against oppression, filled with the sentiments which actuated that grand generation, we seek to restore government of the republic to the hands of the "plain people" with whom it originated.[10]

As progressive populists of today seek national political power, they are starting to discuss how they would reshape the economic and social priorities of the country. The Citizen Action organizations, for instance, have conducted an ongoing dialogue about the economy within their organizations. Thousands attended discussions and debates, took classes or heard lectures. Steve Max, of the Midwest Academy, travelled the country with a slide show, debunking the economic myths that make scapegoats of working people and the poor. Such a process of economic discussion, education, and debate goes far beyond Citizen Action as well. Tens of thousands of people have attended workshops on the Catholic bishops' economic pastoral sponsored by organizations like Valley Interfaith in Texas. In the last two years there have been a number of national conferences on economics attended by a wide range of organizations. Both professionals and working people, some for the first time in their lives, participate in such a process. Economic analysts such as Gar Alperovitz, Jeff Faux, Barry Bluestone, David Gordon, Robert Kuttner, Derek Shearer, and Hazel Henderson have all helped in this effort. Out of this ferment, broad outlines of a populist economic perspective begin to emerge. It serves as a guide to local and national issue campaigns and electoral platforms and as a demonstration of how priorities will change as progressive populists win public office.

A People's Working Economy

The Reagan administration has brought about many significant economic changes. Perhaps the most outstanding is the lowering of inflation from 13 percent in 1979 to 5 percent by February 1986. Much has been said about rising incomes and living standards since 1980. What appears to be actually happening is that the population is splitting more or less evenly down the middle. Those in the top half of the income scale are experiencing a rising standard of living. The wealthier a family is, the faster its living standard has been rising, thanks in part to the administrations' tax policies.[11]

It is significant that in one of the strongest economic recoveries since the Second World War, median family income in 1984 was no higher than it had been in 1979. There were 4.4 million more poor people in 1984 than in 1980 in spite of the rising economy. Economic growth is leaving behind the poorer half of the population, which includes minorities, families with only one wage earner, families headed by women, many of the young "new collar" families who are working in service occupations, rust belt families, and many farm families. There are a large number of families in flux, some moving up, others moving down, and many moving back and forth from year to year. It is the goal of populist economics to restore upward mobility throughout society.

Progressive populist economics has people as its starting point. It says that the well-being of the people is the basic purpose of the economy, not an incidental or dispensable by-product. This judgment is made not only out of moral conviction but also with the knowledge than an economy operated for the benefit of the many will be healthier and more viable than one that strives for the profit of a few.

Ours is often referred to as a consumer or a market economy, one in which enterprises large and small develop to satisfy people's needs. In the course of this, jobs are created and wealth is produced. It follows that the better able people are to satisfy their needs as consumers, the stronger the economy will become. This fact, the basis of the progressive populist economic view, seems self-evident. Yet it is in direct conflict with the prevailing economic wisdom practiced today. Current public policy supports lowering wages, eliminating well-paying jobs from the economy, and cutting programs that increase the purchasing power of the poor. Indeed, the new ideal corporate image is "lean and mean," which usually means cutting payrolls, with the inevitable result that consumers, themselves employees, also become lean and mean. In a system that can produce an abundance of virtually everything and that must operate near capacity to maintain full employment, lean consumers with lean incomes are a threat to economic stability.

The problem is that each corporation would like to pay the lowest possible wages to its own employees but sell its products to other people who make more money working for a different company. This may be good business for the individual corporation. When every business tries to do it, it depresses the whole economy. That is why populism looks at what is good for people first, and at what is good for profits second.

"As wage settlements and salary plans for the next year take shape," said the *New York Times*, "all signs suggest that 1986 will be the fifth consecutive year that the typical American worker will receive a smaller pay increase than in the year before." The fact is that industrial workers' pay is rising more slowly than inflation, which means that many people are losing purchasing power, not gaining it.[12]

While frantic efforts are made to increase American sales abroad, a vast potential market here at home is ignored, a market that would exist if more people had the money to satisfy their needs. The plain fact is that most Americans just don't earn a lot of money. Since 1980, poverty has risen by 15 percent. During the last decade one out of every four Americans spent some time in poverty. One third of all American families are low income by Labor Department standards (this is $16,778 family income for family of four in 1983). Forty-three percent of all senior citizen families are low income. Half of all the children in America are low income. More than half of all black families and half of all Hispanic families are low income. Seventy percent of all families headed by women are low income.[13]

Half of all American families don't even meet the Labor Department standard for being middle class (this is $30,361 family income for family of four; December, 1985). The lowest paying service industries employ forty-four million people whose average income is only fifteen thousand dollars a year. Progressive populism challenges the view that this situation is good for people or good for the economy. It organizes to raise the standard of living through the minimum wage, the union wage, pay equity, comparable worth, minimum food prices for farmers, and raising the safety net for seniors and those unable to work. Strangely, the right wing organizations, while they call for strengthening the family, ending welfare dependence, and increasing the dignity of old age, are completely silent about raising incomes. How can it be otherwise when they have tied themselves to a corporate economic agenda so shortsighted that it sacrifices the long term stability of the economy for a quarterly rise in profits? Citizen organizations are shifting the discussion away from the empty rhetoric of the right and over to the real ways of strengthening the family. Jobs for parents who want to work, with salaries high enough that one parent has the option of staying home with the children, incomes that make it possible for grown children, parents, and grandparents to all live in the same community, salaries and loan programs that ensure children that if they do well in school there is money for college—all such goals are the most effective ways of strengthening the family. All of these are essentially questions of income where the right wing and its elected office holders come up empty handed.[14]

Of course, there is little point in demanding higher wages from corporations that are unable to pay them. Progressive populist principles call for a new relationship between the government and business that will strengthen business and help it to become competitive. The present relationship has amounted to little more than a welfare program for corporations, engendering a sick dependency on such government handouts as cost plus defense contracts, with no limits on cost overruns and no required guarantees that the product will even work. Such practices make corporate executives lazy, sloppy, and, as the exposures at General Dynamics and other defense contractors indicate, prone to crime. The Reagan corporate tax cut bonanza, amounting to roughly $25 billion a year, is another welfare handout with no requirement that the money actually be used for research, development, and production instead of stock speculation and foreign investment. Yet another was the opening of our national forests to private timber and mining interests and the commercial development of national parks. Conservatives need to remember their old bromide: throwing money at problems does more harm than good.[15]

A new economic policy based on progressive populist values will replace across-the-board corporate tax cuts with a carefully targeted investment policy to upgrade both old and new industry. The high tech industry, where 2.5 million jobs are at stake, provides one example of what might be done. *Business Week* noted that "America's High Tech sector will soon be in danger of losing its world leadership position. . . . The basic problem is that U.S. High Tech companies are no longer able to translate their technology into competitive products." An industry study commission headed by Hewlett-Packard president John A. Young, suggested some areas where changes in government policy would improve the situation. The commission said that too little federal money is spent on civilian research and too much (over 50 percent) on the military. In addition, it found that there were not enough engineers graduating from the nation's universities. Many companies, the commission said, needed access to investment capital in order to turn ideas into marketable products, and the industry as a whole required a trade-import policy. The progressive populist approach would have the federal and state governments play a direct and active role in solving these problems. In a number of states, for example, citizen groups are fighting for the establishment of state-owned banks, which can provide start up capital for local entrepreneurs. Other citizen organizations are working for requirements that banks make loans to businesses that will provide local jobs.[16]

These issues prefigure what a national progressive populist economic policy would be like. Public investment in the nation's decaying industrial infrastructure would be greatly increased. Not only would old industries be modernized, but also the latest communication and transportation technologies would be constructed nationally. At the same time, greater investment would be made in the environment because toxic waste and pollution deplete human and natural resources.

Populism opposes the wasteful and irresponsible nature of much current corporate investment policy. Between 1980 and 1984, $380 billion have gone into corporate mergers and hostile takeovers. Hundreds of billions more have gone into stock market manipulation and speculation. This is money that came from corporate profits and tax give-aways. It should have been used instead to raise wages and lower individual taxes as well as for productive investment in business and industry. Populism believes that this wealth, originally produced by working people, is held in trust by the corporations that are obligated to use it wisely and for the benefit of all. Corporations that waste the nation's financial resources must be stopped. Should not a dollar made through useless speculation, which deprives industry of needed capital, be taxed at a higher rate than a dollar made by actually producing something? Shouldn't the tax structure penalize instead of reward a company like U.S. Steel for taking its capital out of steel production, leaving thousands jobless, and using the money to buy Marathon Oil? Once again, the politicians of the right are silent on these issues. They are quick to condemn when a poor person gets welfare and blows it in a crap game, but when corporate rich do the same, not one word![17]

The progressive populist premise that wages must be raised carries with it an obligation to upgrade the quality of labor in return. Here again there is a positive role for federal and state governments to play in supporting education through the schools as well as through grants for in-plant training. One way to offset the competitive disadvantage of high wages is for America to have the best educated, most skilled, and most productive workforce in the world. Here, too, for all its talk about traditional values, the right wing is working in the opposite direction, organizing local taxpayer insurgencies to slash school budgets while encouraging the administration to cut federal aid and student loans. Progressive populist groups argue for real involvement by parents, students, and teachers in educational policy with funds adequate for quality education.

The progressive populist economic perspective, in summary, sees an increased role for government in helping American business to help itself, but on the basis of accountability to the public well-being. In exchange, corporations profiting from government assistance or contracts are obligated to meet high standards of wages and affirmative action, to respect environmental and safety codes as well as labor laws, and to allow employees and communities a role in decision making. When public money or employee pension funds are used to help corporations, the progressive populist view holds that the community and the employees should become part owners, receiving stock like any other investor would.

Conventional economists of many different political persuasions hold similar viewpoints on the problem of foreign imports. They suggest that America should compete with low foreign wages by lowering its own wages and by eliminating as much labor as possible through automation. From the progressive populist perspective, none of these solutions is particularly helpful. A Korean auto worker, making cars for the American market, gets paid $2.16 an hour in wages and benefits compared to over twenty dollars in the United States. This in part explains why Asian goods flood American markets instead of Asian markets. Few Asian workers can afford to buy the products they make. By the same token, neither can American industrial robots buy the products they make. The dream of a workerless factory is a help only when people can find other jobs at comparable high wages. Progressive populists support industrial development in the Third World and efficient technology in American factories. But new technologies and development must be undertaken in ways that benefit local economies.[18]

Citizen Action organizations see raising Third World living standards as the long term key to the import problem. Higher Third World wages would create local markets for local products as well as for some American exports. More important from the American point of view, it would start to equalize the foreign wage gap. Citizen Action activists speak of a "full employment foreign policy" aimed at raising Third World living standards. They point to the South Korean cars that are starting to show up on the American market and note that one reason for South Korean wages being four dollars an hour is that Korean labor leaders are in prison, kept there by a repressive government supported by American aid and arms. This pattern is repeated in different ways in many parts of the world. Instead of encouraging progressive governments and trade union organizations that will force multinational corporations to pay higher taxes and wages in the Third World, the United States all too often supports oppressive regimes that guarantee the most favorable conditions and cheapest labor not only to our competitors but also to runaway American industry. A full employment foreign policy is based on a different conception of where our real interests lie.

Obviously, raising Third World livings is a very long term solution, but more immediate actions can be taken to improve the trade balance and the import problem. One is the passage of domestic content laws broader than the one on automobiles that has passed the House of Representatives. Such laws require that products sold in America have a certain percentage of parts made in America. Over thirty-two countries have domestic content laws, so their passage here could hardly be called economic aggression.

Community organizations and citizen groups in recent years have come to see the concrete linkages between unbridled military spending and the decay of cities, the loss of family farms, the impoverishment of growing numbers of citizens. "A lot of us in the Populist Caucus are veterans," says populist co-chair Lane Evans, congressman from Illinois. "We know people whose names are on that wall at the Vietnam memorial. We're not alienated from the flag." But Evans, like other progressive populists, is a staunch opponent of a foreign policy that he believes is too interventionist and militarist. Senator Tom Harkin likens the issue to one's family. "How can you say you love your kids and not care how they behave?" [19]

In a populist, working economy, minimum wages would be sufficient to ensure every working American a livelihood of dignity and plenty, every citizen would be guaranteed meaningful, productive work, and support for small businesses would be far greater. Unions' rights to organize, bargain, and protect employees would be firmly guaranteed.

Worker health and safety and the protection of the community from any toxic materials would be central priorities—no more concealed behind the outrageous attempts by many corporations to put a dollar amount on human life. Low cost public transportation, decentralized energy conservation programs, more prudent land use, and renovation of older structures would save considerable fuel. The nation would make major efforts to base energy usage upon renewable sources like solar energy and wind. Questions of appropriate scale technology and community participation in decision making about a range of business issues, from the introduction of new equipment to pollution control, or the tradeoffs for public support for business in areas like capital improvements would become an accustomed part of what "economics" included.

In a populist economy, the ideal farming unit would be a family-size operation, farmed with care for long term health of the land. Nowhere is the absurdity of the present economic relationships more clearly demonstrated than in the farm crisis. Thousands of farmers lose their land every month. Lives and a way of life are being destroyed. When these problems exist in most parts of the world, it is because farmers cannot produce enough food. In America it is because they produce too much. Our economic relations have turned an abundance of food from a blessing into a curse. So much food is produced that to sell it all the price must come down. Even then, the family farm doesn't get the income to pay its debts. Unfortunately, the consumer doesn't even get the benefit of low farm prices because the "middle men"—the processors, packagers, shippers, and distributors—keep prices and profits high. Only when some natural disaster like a frost or a drought destroys a large portion of the crop are farmers able to get an adequate return for what they produce.

A progressive populist farm program includes a required minimum price for farm products. The concept is like the minimum wage for workers. Farmers would be assured of a price sufficient to actually cover their costs and loan payments. A monopoly on the land is greatly to be feared. To prevent agriculture from becoming a system of mega-farms owned by multinational corporations, laws are needed to discourage the entrance of non-family farm corporations into agriculture. A moratorium on farm forclosures and a refinancing of the farm debt will help to keep the family farmer in business.

Farm owners and farm labor don't always have the same interests. Legislation to save the family farm should also recognize the right of agricultural labor to organize, to work under safe, sanitary conditions, and to be fairly paid.

Progressive populist vision informs economic policy in far more ways than these examples. It is developing, not as an abstract economic theory, but as a distillation of actual organizational experience. It is different from simply being a shopping list of good ideas. Right now people work to win most of the measures suggested here and many others that are compatible with the underlying progressive populist values.

Populism places on the national agenda far ranging questions about how our working lives should be structured in the future. It does not assume that present arrangements are the natural order of things. It says that people have the ability to decide how they would like to live their lives and that everything from the length of the working day to the dimensions of private ownership is subject to reevaluation. More deeply, statements like those in the draft of the Catholic bishops's pastoral letter on the economy, calling for a recognition of the dignity of labor and for action "on the side of those who are powerless or on the margins of society," suggest the value discussions that should inform and inspire a far ranging public discussion of our basic goals in economics and the way a future society should be shaped.

The progressive populist economic viewpoint is rooted in the needs of communities. But because much of the implementation must come at the state and national levels, local organizations are increasingly drawn into the electoral arena. It is there that confrontation with corporate and right wing power takes place. The progressive populist economic viewpoint is therefore both a plan for what can happen after the electoral victory of a coalition of progressive forces and a description of the day to day organizing that are the building blocks of that coalition. The experiences and skills gained in organizing locally prepare people for larger, national campaigns and help them identify the issues on which national coalitions are built.

Toward a Working Democracy and a Working Society

A populist government supports self-reliance through the democratic organization of people. It seeks, not to replace local structures by a centralized bureaucracy, but to push to the limit our capacity to experiment with democracy. The progressive populist government will slash meaningless regulations, do away with ridiculous paperwork. But it is activist: in the economy it will intervene, not to promote special interests, but to curb abuses, invest in our future through education, and always be guided by principles supporting the voluntary self-organization of our people.

Progressive populist democratic values like economic values are both the rationale for the issue and electoral organizing efforts now in progress and the basis of our vision of what the future could be like after the victory of the progressive populist movement.

"Democracy *means* that politicians are the people's servants," explained Sonia Hernandez, a leader in the San Antonio community group, COPS, which has transformed political relations in the city and given poor and working people a voice for the first time. Progressive populist politics has long expressed the belief that government is neither the problem, as conventional conservatism has it, nor the solution, as traditional liberalism tends to view it. Neither is government a neutral arbitrator of social disputes. Indeed, progressive populism sees the main dynamic of present American politics as a contest over whose interests government will serve—those of the corporate rich or those of the majority of the people. It is only in government that the power exists to control and direct the multinational corporations that have set their own economic agenda quite apart from the interests of any one country or people.[20]

In recent years, local initiative and state and national coalitions across the country have revived the idea that government should provide tools and resources so people can become knowledgeable and effective citizens and be able to renew their communities. But in this view, government does not seek to impose uniformity or standardization. It recognizes the diversity of American communities as its greatest source of social creativity and energy.

Our nation run on progressive populist principles would mean the reinvigoration of federalism to strengthen local levels of government. Citizens' right of access to knowledge and information and their widespread input into every form of government decision would be guaranteed. Traditions like the New England town meeting would revive. Strict funding limits on elections would be be implemented, and, perhaps, public subsidy for political campaigns would be instituted. Large numbers of citizens would gain experience in public affairs. Citizenship as a continuing obligation and its appropriate skills and values would become central parts of educational curricula, taught at every level.[21]

In the earliest expressions of American democratic philosophy, civic involvement was regarded as the foundation of free society—indeed, as the only way in which active public life, personal and communal responsibility, and the broader commonwealth could be renewed and sustained. "What country can preserve its liberties if their rulers are not warned from time to time that their people preserve the spirit of resistance?" wrote Thomas Jefferson in *Notes on the State of Virginia*. Citizen activism of recent years renews and enriches this venerable philosophy. The most successful examples of citizen activism combine effective issue work with broad coalitions among diverse groups. And, increasingly, citizen action takes on broader cultural dimensions as well, with cultural celebrations, history projects, value discussions, and the like as integral parts. In the 1980s and 1990s, democratic civic involvements promote an expanded role for those who have been excluded from full participation, in the process redefining terms like "community" and "leadership." It sees our traditions of family, faith, neighborhood, ethnic heritage, craft and work, voluntary organizations, and the like as a richly pluralist, dynamic, and changing heritage.[22]

A future that witnessed a renewed spirit of civic responsibility would also see a vital process of moral renewal, away from the radical individualism and dog-eat-dog morality too often enshrined in the mass culture today. These are reflections of the values of corporate culture. They are the ways that large corporations often act toward each other and toward their employees, projected outward as the standard for the whole society. Reducing the economic and political power of the large corporations in our country will make possible movement toward a balance of individual interests and communal commitments. It would entail a renewed attachment to values of community and family, principles of life long learning, concern for frugality, care for resources, and attention to quality that once characterized American life. Concepts of self-help, preventive medicine, and more emphasis on lay participation in every form of social service would be central. Ordinary people could live with a sense of security, knowing that the loss of a job, an illness, or simply growing old would not bring catastrophe to them and their families. A revitalization of smaller scale institutions would parallel, though not replace, large structures.[23]

The Promise of Democratic Populism

As these pages have testified, progressive populist citizen action organizing brings about personal and political transformation. Most people receive recognition only twice in their lives: when they are born and when they die. Citizen organizing makes celebrities out of many ordinary people and heroes of a few. It transforms people's lives. It brings out the collective power that they have to change events large and small. It creates a collective voice for those who would otherwise go unheard. It teaches people that they can confront those who are highly placed, better educated, more powerful, or richer than themselves and win. It confirms things that people knew in their hearts to be right, although the "experts" tried to convince them that they were wrong. It teaches people that they can trust their own judgment, that they can understand complex issues, that they are entitled to have opinions, and that their opinions are valuable.

Through organization, people learn alternatives to lives of quiet desperation and worry. They come to see that what appeared to be their private troubles are parts of larger patterns affecting thousands or millions of others. They learn the skills of writing, speaking, managing large enterprises and multimillion dollar budgets, running political campaigns, and holding politicians accountable to the people's will. In short, through organizing, ordinary people come to possess the skills and abilities that those with education or wealth have always taken for granted. It creates new organizations and revitalizes old ones. It organizes the unorganized and assembles coalitions locally and nationally.

Citizen organizing has taken on the challenge of fashioning one movement out of many races, cultures, and religions. It contends daily in its own ranks with the prejudices and hatreds built up over centuries. It is determined that these will not forever be the divisive tools that have allowed the lives of so many to be dominated by so few.

Citizen organizing speaks for justice, challenging corporate greed and power from the mightiest multinational oil company to the smallest toxic disposal company. It knows no parochial bounds of issue or geography but goes into combat wherever people are willing to fight so that justice will be done.

The citizens movement is open to all who want to improve their lives, to all those who value their families, their communities, their nation, and the world, to all who believe that together they can make a difference. It is built on the proud heritage of those who have gone before them. And it is dedicated to those who will come after.

NOTES

PRELUDE

1. Don Wiener interview with Robert Bagley, Dec. 20, 1985, Castlewood, Mo.

2. Figures on corporate contributions, "Story of Superfund Reauthorization Campaign," *The Maine Alliance*, Winter, 1985.

CHAPTER ONE

Epigraph: Jerry Falwell, Introduction, in Richard A. Viguerie, *The New Right: We're Ready to Lead* (Falls Church, Va.: Viguerie, 1980).

1. On the history and various dimensions of the New Right, see, as a sampling, Robert Cooney, "The Public Interest Suffers Most: Exploiters of Fear Warp National Debate," *Viewpoint* 8, no. 2 (Spring, 1978); James Kilpatrick, "The Good Old Tide of Conservatism," *Nation's Business*, Dec. 1978; Viguerie, *New Right*; "Preachers in Politics," *U.S. News and World Report*, Sept. 15, 1980; *U.S. News and World Report* cover story, Nov. 17, 1980; Wayne King, "Right Wing Extremists Seek to Recruit Farmers," *New York Times*, Sept. 20, 1985; Leon Friedman, "Don't Meddle with Habeas Corpus," *New York Times*, Dec. 3, 1985; Cameron Johnson, *Raleigh News and Observer*, July 21, 1975; Reagan quoted in George Will, "The Real Campaign of 1984," *Newsweek*, Sept. 2, 1985.

2. Descriptions of the growth of progressive citizen activism are available from a number of sources. See, for instance, Harry C. Boyte, *The Backyard Revolution: Understanding the New Citizen Movement* (Philadelphia: Temple University Press, 1980); Studs Terkel, "Across America There's a Flowing of Life's Juices," *Parade*, Oct. 12, 1980; John Herbers, "Grass Roots Groups Go National," *New York Times Magazine*, Sept. 4, 1983; Nancy Shulins, "Backyard Rebellion: Neighborhoods Dig In and Fight City Hall," Associated Press feature, reprinted in *St. Paul Pioneer Press* and elsewhere, Jan. 29, 1984; "The Revival of Populism," *Congressional Quarterly*, April 21, 1984, p. 913.

3. Paul Weyrich quoted in Viguerie, *New Right*, p. 42.

4. *Ibid.*, pp. 42–44.

5. *Ibid.*, pp. 122–24.

6. Mickey Edwards quoted in "Battle Cries from the New Right," *Viewpoint* 8, no. 2 (Spring, 1978): 15.

7. Viguerie, *New Right*, p. 122.

8. *Ibid.*, p. 84; Billy James Hargis and the National Conservative Political Action Committee quoted in "Battle Cries," *Viewpoint*, p. 15.

9. For a deft discussion of the decline of liberalism in the 1960s, see Allen J. Matusow, *The Unraveling of America: A History of Liberalism in the 1960s* (New York: Harper & Row, 1984).

10. Figures on home ownership from Walter Dean Burnham, "The Eclipse of the Democratic Party," *Democracy*, July, 1982, p. 11.

11. Thurman Arnold quoted in Howard Zinn, "Middle Class America Refurbished," in Allen Davis and Harold Woodman, eds., *Conflict and Consensus in American History* (Lexington, Mass.: D.C. Heath, 1972), p. 306; see also, for instance, Samuel Hays, "The Politics of Reform in Municipal Government in the Progressive Era," in Stanley Kutz and Stanley Kutler, eds., *New Perspectives on the American Past* (Boston: Little, Brown, 1969). On changing liberal meanings of democracy, see, for instance, Henry Kariel, ed., *Frontiers of Democratic Theory* (New York: Random House, 1970); Boyte, *Backyard Revolution*; Sara Evans and Harry C. Boyte, *Free Spaces: The Sources of Democratic Change in America* (New York: Harper & Row, 1986).

12. White ethnics quoted in Glenn Lowry, "A Crisis Grows in Brooklyn," *The New Republic*, Sept. 9, 1985, p. 32; Kevin Phillips quoted in John Judis, "The New Right Wins Battle of Ideas," *In These Times*, April 19, 1978.

13. George Wallace quoted in Viguerie, *New Right*, pp. 32–33, 219–20, and Matusow, *Unraveling of America*, pp. 422–26.

14. On mainstream liberal economic views, see Henry Owen and Charles L. Schultze, eds., *Setting National Priorities: The Next Ten Years* (Washington, D.C.: Brookings Institution, 1976); on increasing domination of Democrats by corporate finances and Carter's tax policies, in part as consequence, see David Osborne, "The Permanent Party," *Mother Jones*, Aug.–Sept., 1984, pp. 21–47; see also Robert Kuttner, "Ass Backwards," *The New Republic*, April 22, 1985; President's Commission for a National Agenda for the Eighties, *Urban America in the Eighties: Perspectives and Prospects* (Washington, D.C.: USGPO, 1980), p. 100: Alan Greenspan quoted in Joseph Kraft, "Problems Carter Inherited," *Minneapolis Tribune*, Jan. 20, 1977.

15. Housewife quoted in Gar Alperovitz and Jeff Faux, *Rebuilding America: A Blueprint for the New Economy* (New York: Pantheon, 1984), p. 168.

16. Hazel Haralson Redding quoted in John Herbers, "Small-Town America: A Portrait," *New York Times Magazine*, Dec. 10, 1978, pp. 190, 192; woman from Iowa quoted in John Herbers, "Dispute in Iowa Attests to Ebbing Confidence in U.S. Domestic Programs," *New York Times*, Dec. 14, 1979; see also

Minneapolis Tribune poll, April 6, 1980; *Newsweek* cover story, "Is America Turning Right?" Nov. 7, 1977; "Why the Shift to Conservatism?," *U.S. News and World Report*, Jan. 23, 1978; Carl Holman quoted in *Minneapolis Tribune*, Nov. 4, 1985.

17. On prejudice, Harris poll, Feb. 21, 1979, and Gallup poll, Nov. 23, 1978; on values, Gallup poll, Jan. 14, 1982; on voluntarism, Gallup poll, Dec. 1, 1978 —all from *Minneapolis Tribune*.

18. Mildred Bailey quoted in *Raleigh News and Observer*, July 21, 1975; polling on corporations by Peter Hart, reported in *North Carolina Anvil*, Sept. 13, 1975.

19. Reagan speech quoted in William Schambra, *The Quest for Community and the Quest for a New Public Philosophy* (Washington, D.C.: American Enterprise Institute, 1983), p. 30; Hedrick Smith, "Reagan's Populist Coalition," *New York Times*, March 6, 1980; *Washington Post*, Nov. 19, 1979; *New York Times*, April 12, 1980.

20. Will, "Real Campaign of 1984"; Reagan quoted in Schambra, *Quest for Community*, pp. 32-33; also quoted in *New York Times*, Aug. 20, 1985; Richard Darman, "Historic Tax Reform: The Populist Correction," speech to the Institute for Research on the Economics of Taxation, April 15, 1985, Washington, D.C.

21. John Winthrop quoted in Robert Bellah, *The Broken Covenant: American Civil Religion in a Time of Trial* (New York: Seabury, 1975), p. 15.

22. Boyte interview with Gary Hattem, March 15, 1982, New York. For a description of the way the Reagan administration branded as potentially subversive and dangerous even moderate to conservative blue collar community organizations, see, for instance, *Kansas City Star*, Jan. 3, 1982; Harry C. Boyte, "Ronald Reagan and America's Neighborhoods," in Frank Riessman, Colin Greer, and Alan Gartner, eds., *What Reagan Is Doing to Us* (New York: Harper & Row, 1982), pp. 109-24; see also *Neighborhood: The Journal for City Preservation*, Dec., 1978. On Fattah and Umoja, see William Robbins, "Philadelphia Opens Home to Ex-Gang Members," *New York Times*, Nov. 5, 1981; Harry C. Boyte, "Reagan vs. the Neighborhoods," *Social Policy* 12, no. 4 (Spring, 1982): 7-8.

23. Barbara Mikulski, "A Populist, Feminist and Progressive," in Harry C. Boyte and Frank Riessman, eds., *Populism Today: The Politics of Empowerment* (Philadelphia: Temple University Press, 1986).

24. Brian O'Connell quoted in *New York Times*, Jan. 24, 1985; Neal Peirce quoted in *Minneapolis Tribune*, Jan. 22, 1984. For an analysis along these lines, see also Robert Bellah et al., *Habits of the Heart: Individualism and Commitment in American Life* (Berkeley: University of California Press, 1985).

25. On contrasting views of the sources of the American democratic traditions (variously, the republican ideological tradition reaching through the Italian Renaissance and the Country Party in England, on the one hand, and the tradi-

tion of Rousseau, on the other), sec, for instance, J. G. A. Pocock, *The Machiavellian Moment: Florentine Political Thought and Democratic Theory* (Princeton: Princeton University Press, 1975), and James Miller, *Rousseau: Dreamer of Democracy* (New Haven: Yale University Press, 1983); for a discussion of the commonwealth in American history, see Harry C. Boyte, *Community Is Possible: Repairing America's Roots* (New York: Harper & Row, 1984); on the Reagan administration's assault on the commonwealth, see, for instance, Jim Fain, "Luxury and Limos for the Glittering Gucci Set," *Minneapolis Tribune*, Dec. 1, 1985; "For Sale: Uncle Sam," *Newsweek*, Dec. 30, 1985.

26. Alan Brinkley, "Richard Hofstadter's *The Age of Reform*: A Reconsideration," *Reviews in American History* 13, no. 3 (Sept., 1985): 467; for an extended treatment of populism's cultural dynamics, see Lawrence Goodwyn, *Democratic Promise: The Populist Moment in American History* (New York: Oxford University Press, 1976).

27. Evans and Boyte, *Free Spaces.*

CHAPTER TWO

Epigraph: Massachusetts Fair Share/Citizen Action, "To Protect Our Families, Neighborhoods, and Standards of Living," program, 1982, Boston, p. 3.

1. Boyte interview with Tom Harkin, April 30, 1985, Washington, D.C.

2. Boyte interview with Chuck Deppert, Aug. 3, 1985, Chicago.

3. Story of Philip Frazeur from Colman McCarthy, "Gas Bill Rebellion," *Washington Post*, March 4, 1984.

4. Story of Randall Carson farm from Andrew Malcolm, "Farmers and Unions Joining to Fight Economic Hardship," *New York Times*, June 5, 1983.

5. Story of Cora Tucker drawn from Boyte interview with Ron Charity, Sept. 16, 1985, Richmond, Va.; *Halifax News and Record*, Feb. 1, 1983.

6. Interview with Charles Williams, April 26, 1985, Chicago; others quoted in Malcolm, "Farmers and Unions."

7. For useful discussions of this ideological tradition, see, for instance, Vernon Louis Parrington, *Main Currents in American Thought: An Interpretation of American Literature from the Beginnings to 1920* (New York: Harcourt, Brace and Co., 1927); Leon Fink, *Workingmen's Democracy: The Knights of Labor and American Politics* (Urbana: University of Illinois Press, 1983).

8. *Business Week*, Oct. 12, 1974; on the decline in productivity relative to other nations, see, for instance, Robert Reich and Ira Magaziner, *Minding America's Business: The Decline and Rise of the American Economy* (New York: Harcourt Brace Jovanovich, 1982), pp. 30, 36; world trade figures, AFL-CIO, "Economic Policy Committee Report," in Sumner M. Rosen, ed., *Economic Power Failure: The Current American Crisis* (New York: McGraw-Hill,

1975), p. 114; see also Joyce Kolko, *America and the Crisis of World Capitalism* (Boston: Beacon Press, 1974), pp. 4–25.

9. Reich and Magaziner, *Minding America's Business*, pp. 56, 155, 160–61; see also Robert H. Hayes and William J. Abernathy, "Managing Our Way to Economic Decline," *Harvard Business Review*, July–Aug., 1980; on alternatives, Gar Alperovitz and Jeff Faux, *Rebuilding America: A Blueprint for the New Economy* (New York: Pantheon, 1984), pp. 100–104; Mobil ad number 4, "The Free Market: Radicalism for the 1980s," published in *New York Times* and elsewhere, 1978.

10. Milton Mayer, *The Money Bazaars: Understanding the Banking Revolution Around Us* (New York: E. P. Dutton, 1984), p. 233; on speculation, see, for instance, Reich and Magaziner, *Minding America's Business*, pp. 116–17; executive recruiter quoted in Alperovitz and Faux, *Rebuilding America*, p. 98.

11. On concentration, see Alperovitz and Faux, *Rebuilding America*, p. 34.

12. Neal Peirce, "Reagan Fails to Aid New Small Business," *Minneapolis Tribune*, March 29, 1981; figures on small business job production from Neal Peirce, "Smokestack Chasing Myths," *Minneapolis Tribune*, March 29, 1981; figures on small business job production from Neal Peirce, "Smokestack Chasing Myths," *Minneapolis Tribune*, June 3, 1979; John Cavanagh, "The Big Get Bigger," *USA Today*, Oct. 13, 1983.

13. *Business Week*, Aug. 13, 1984.

14. Tom Medved and George Papson quoted in *Newsweek* special issue, "Left Out: The Human Cost of the Collapse of Industrial America," March 21, 1983.

15. Bruce Springsteen, "Born in the U.S.A."

16. The 83 percent figure includes, under service, transportation and utility workers who make more an hour than do workers in manufacturing as well as workers in the wholesale trade who make 93 percent of the manufacturing wage. On the other hand, workers in finance, insurance, and real estate earn an average weekly wage that is equal to only 75 percent of the manufacturing wage. In business and health services it is 68 percent and in the retail trade only 46 percent. Thus, as of September 1985, retail workers averaged $177.90 a week compared to $389.23 in manufacturing (Council on International and Public Affairs, Special Report 5, Nov. 1985; based on BLS figures).

17. Consequences of absentee ownership and mergers, see Alperovitz and Faux, *Rebuilding America*, especially pp. 96–99; "The Age of Cowboy Capitalism," *Newsweek*, May 13, 1985; "USA Must Keep Manufacturing to Stay Abreast of Technology," *USA Today*, April 26, 1985; see also "The Raider Barons," *U.S. News and World Report*, April 8, 1985; Robert Collier, "Democratizing the Private Sector," *Socialist Review*, Spring, 1985, pp. 41–63. On loss of industrial jobs and shift to service, see Barry Bluestone, "The Destructive Effects of Capital Mobility," *Minnesota Leader*, April–May, 1983; "Jobs," *Minneapolis*

Tribune, May 21, 1985. On changing patterns in work, see Ward Morehouse and David Dembo, *The Underbelly of the U.S. Economy: Joblessness and Pauperization of Work in America* (New York: Council on International and Public Affairs, 1985), Special Reports 2 and 3, pp. 12–13, 10–11; Villers Foundation, *America's Future Is Ours to Build* (Washington, D.C.: Villers, 1983); Joint Congressional Committee Report, *Minneapolis Tribune,* Nov. 31, 1985. On increases in upper income, see Morehouse and Dembo, *Underbelly of the U.S. Economy,* Report 3.

18. Barbara Mikulski, in Harry C. Boyte and Frank Riessman, eds., *Populism Today: The Politics of Empowerment* (Philadelphia: Temple University Press, 1986).

CHAPTER THREE

Epigraph: *Citizen Action News,* Spring, 1980.

1. Mark Moller-Gunderson quoted in Janet Kelsey, "Citizen Action: Making Democracy Work," *Citizen Action News,* Spring, 1983; Booth interview with Marie Clark, May 1, 1985, Chicago.

2. The material on Chuck Deppert is from Boyte interview with Deppert, Aug. 3, 1985, Chicago; also *Citizen Action News,* Spring, 1983.

3. The material on Cora Tucker is from Boyte interviews with Tucker, March 12, 1985, Washington, D.C.; April 20, 1985, Chicago; *Citizen Action News,* Spring, 1985; Citizens for a Better America, *A Ten Year Report* (Halifax, Va.: Citizens for a Better America, 1985).

4. The material on Doreen Del Bianco is from Boyte interview with Del Bianco, Aug. 2, 1985, Chicago; *Citizen Action News* interview, Fall, 1982.

5. Boyte interview with Lynn Cardiff, Aug. 2, 1985, Chicago.

6. Boyte interview with Bob Hudek, April 27, 1985, Chicago.

7. Boyte interview with Bill Thompson, April 18, 1977, Boston.

8. Citizen Action Program described in Derek Shearer, "CAP: New Breeze in the Windy City," *Ramparts,* Oct., 1973, pp. 12–16; Harry C. Boyte, *Backyard Revolution: Understanding the New Citizen Movement* (Philadelphia: Temple University Press, 1980); Midwest Academy, *Training Manual* (Chicago: Midwest Academy, 1974); Booth interview with Steve Max, Aug. 1, 1985, Chicago; on the changing context of organizing, see also Robert Fisher, *Let the People Decide: Neighborhood Organizing in America* (Boston: T. K. Hall, 1984), especially chap. 5, "The New Populism of the 1970s."

9. Boyte interview with Ellen Cassedy, April 17, 1977, Somerville, Mass.

10. Boyte interview with Robert Creamer, April 26, 1985, Chicago; Boyte interview with Jackie Kendall, April 25, 1985, Chicago; Marie Clay, "Seniors

in the Eighties," *Citizen Action News*, July–Aug., 1980; Joe Ruiz quoted in Lenora Davis, "UNO: Building a New Future," *Citizen Action News*, Summer, 1981.

11. Kendall interview.

12. Boyte interviews with Ira Arlook, Nov. 12, 1977, Washington, D.C.; March 13, 1985, Washington, D.C.; Aug. 1, 1985; Chicago.

13. Boyte interview with Robert Brandon, March 11, 1985, Washington, D.C.

14. CLEC early history in Arn Pearson, "Resource Mobilization in the 1980s: A Case Study of the Citizen Labor Energy Coalition," senior thesis, Cornell University, 1984, pp. 46–48; Booth interview with William Hutton, May 1, 1985, Chicago.

15. Boyte interview with Don Wiener, Aug. 2, 1985, Chicago; Wiener also quoted in Pearson, "Resource Mobilization," p. 93; description of state-national relations, pp. 47–48.

16. Boyte interview with Tami Odell, March 13, 1985, Washington, D.C.

17. Citizen Action strategy described in Bob Hudek, *Citizen Action Strategy* (Chicago: Midwest Academy, 1983); Boyte interview with Jeff Eagan and Al Levie, Dec. 10, 1985, Milwaukee.

18. Boyte interview with Max Rossman, Dec. 13, 1985, Seattle.

19. Booth interview with Rochelle Davis, March 1, 1986, Chicago.

20. Boyte interview with Si Kahn, Aug. 1, 1985, Chicago.

21. Boyte interview with Sandra McArthur, Aug. 14, 1985, Collegeville, Minn.

CHAPTER FOUR

Epigraph: Si Kahn, canvass song, © 1982.

1. Description of Linda Haese drawn from first-hand impressions and discussions with Boyte, June 11, 1985, North St. Paul.

2. These observations were drawn from Booth discussions at canvass conference in Cleveland, July 4, 1984.

3. Boyte interview with Marc Anderson, Sept. 20, 1985, Minneapolis.

4. Remarkably little has been written on the canvass, though it is a communications technique that may well hold political potential equal to or greater than the direct mail techniques that have been analyzed in some detail. One rare overview is found in Larry Marx, "Taking the Message Door to Door," *Citizen Action News*, Spring, 1983; for descriptions of its *impact*, see, for instance, John Herbers, "Canvassers Hope to Reach 15 Million on Energy Costs," *New York Times*, March 27, 1983; "Chemical Hazards Generate Coalition for Stronger Laws," *Washington Post*, Feb. 14, 1984.

5. Boyte interview with Larry Marx, June 21, 1985, St. Paul.

6. Boyte canvass discussions, June 11, 1985, St. Paul.

7. This and the following paragraph based on Boyte observations of canvass office, June 11, 1985, St. Paul.

8. Boyte interview with George Knotek, June 7, 1985, St. Paul, Minn.

9. *Ibid.*

10. Boyte interview with Pam Bemis, Oct. 17, 1985, Worchester, Mass.

11. This and the following two paragraphs based on Boyte interview with Barbara Helmick, June 21, 1985, St. Paul.

12. Boyte Anderson interview; Helmick interview.

13. Boyte interview with Naya Pyskacek and Chris Williams, Feb. 17, 1985, New York and Bloomington, Ind.

14. Boyte interview with Peter Rawson, Oct. 17, 1985, Hartford, Conn.

15. Marx interview.

16. Boyte interview with Liz Blackburn, Feb. 10, 1986, Washington, D.C.

17. Booth interview with Sophie Ann Aoki, Aug. 1, 1985, Washington, D.C.

18. Marx interview; Washington woman, quoted in Fair Share *Fair Share*, Dec., 1983.

19. Helmick interview.

20. *Ibid.*

21. Boyte interview with Tom Asher, Sept. 1985, Washington, D.C.

22. Boyte interview with Sue Jashinsky, Aug. 2, 1985, Chicago; Boyte interview with Mike Podhorzer, March 11, 1985, Washington, D.C.

23. Marx interview; Jashinsky interview; Boyte interview with Vicki Sipe, Aug. 2, 1985, Chicago.

24. Boyte interview with David Zwick, Aug. 2, 1985, Chicago; Boyte interview with Diane Jensen, June 21, 1985, Minneapolis.

25. Marx interview.

26. Jashinsky interview.

27. Boyte interview with Jessica Hallowell, Oct. 17, 1985, Boston; Sipe interview; Helmick interview.

CHAPTER FIVE

1. Description and quotations from Brad Karkkainen, "Showdown in Chicago," *Citizen Action News*, Fall, 1981.

2. Robert Creamer, quoted in *Los Angeles Times*, Dec. 26, 1982; Booth interview with Creamer, Sept. 1, 1983, Chicago.

3. *Christian Science Monitor*, Dec. 23, 1977.

4. The making of the oil empire is described in Robert Engler, *The Politics of Oil: Private Power and Democratic Directions* (Chicago: University of Chicago Press, 1967); patterns of concentration described in Ford Foundation Energy

Policy Project, *A Time to Choose: America's Energy Future* (Cambridge, Mass.: Ballinger, 1974), especially pp. 231, 233; energy lobbying, Pietro Nivola, "Energy Policy and the Congress: The Politics of the Natural Gas Policy Act of 1978," *Public Policy* 28, no. 4 (1979): 491–543.

5. The history of the natural gas debate is described well in Arn Pearson, "Resource Mobilization in the 1980s: A Case Study of the Citizen/Labor Energy Coalition," senior thesis, Cornell University, 1984, pp. 26–32; James Halverson's warnings described in Robert Sherrill, "The Case Against the Oil Companies," in Mark Green and Robert Massie, Jr., eds., *Big Business Reader: Essays on Corporate America* (New York: Pilgrim, 1980), p. 30.

6. Sherrill, "Case Against the Oil Companies," p. 32.

7. Philadelphia woman and Kansas Farmer from CLEC hearing documents, Big Oil Day, 1979.

8. Pearson, "Resource Mobilization," pp. 35, 37, 40, 44.

9. Heather Booth and William Winpisinger, quoted in Pearson, "Resource Mobilization," p. 84; Booth interview with Winpisinger, May 1, 1985; Booth Big Oil speech, in CLEC files, Chicago.

10. Big Oil Day activities described in Pearson, "Resource Mobilization," pp. 47–48.

11. Bill Moore, interviewed in *Citizen Action News*, Summer, 1981; Larry Converse, quoted in *Citizen Action News*, Spring, 1981.

12. Dan Kaemmerer, "Citizen Action Is Born in Wisconsin," *Citizen Action News*, Fall, 1982.

13. This and the following six paragraphs based on interview with Kenneth Montague, Aug. 3, 1985, Chicago; description of meeting with BG&E also from Boyte interview with Sue Jashinsky, Aug. 2, 1985, Chicago.

14. Listing of groups in Citizen Labor Energy Coalition, "A History of the Citizen Labor Energy Coalition," Spring, 1983, p. 5.

15. Michael Halbouty, quoted in *Citizen Action News*, Summer, 1981.

16. Rob Bauman, "Citizen Action Fighting to Stop Decontrol," *Citizen Action News*, Summer, 1981; Brad Karkkainen, "Reagan Drops Gas Decontrol Plan, Threat of Backdoor Decontrol Seen," *Citizen Action News*, Winter, 1982.

17. Booth interview with Robert Brandon, February 10, 1986, Washington, D.C.

18. Booth interview with Miles Rubin, March 11, 1985, Washington, D.C.; Pearson, "Resource Mobilization," pp. 50–51.

19. CLEC staff memo, "Brief Analysis of the Impact of the Campaign to Stop Natural Gas Decontrol," Oct. 11, 1982, p. 2.

20. Pearson, "Resource Mobilization," pp. 51–52.

21. Boyte interview with Mike Podhorzer, March 11, 1985, Washington, D.C.; Pearson, "Resource Mobilization," p. 52–53.

22. Jashinsky interview; interview with Pat Englert, Aug. 2, 1985, Chicago.

23. Pearson, "Resource Mobilization," p. 54.

24. Electoral campaigns described in CLEC, "History"; Brad Karkkainen, "Election Results Will Decide Natural Gas Price Policy," *Citizen Action News*, Summer, 1982.

25. Pearson, "Resource Mobilization," pp. 57–63.

The major oil companies today try to discredit CLEC by saying it was wrong about its predictions regarding decontrol. Since 1982, oil prices have been falling. The combination of serious oil-price-induced recession and increasing surplus throughout the world, rather than decontrol, have been the driving force. Because natural gas in the United States competes with oil, its prices have also been dropping. Despite a decline of ten dollars a barrel since 1981, oil prices are still over six times the price in 1973, before international events drove oil from three to twelve dollars a barrel.

26. *Ibid.*, p. 64; Winpisinger interview.

27. Brandon interview.

CHAPTER SIX

1. This and the following paragraph based on "Can It Happen Here?," *Newsweek* cover story, Dec. 17, 1984.

2. Booth discussions with West Virginia Citizen Action, May, 1985.

3. *Ibid.*; story of leak in August from "America's Toxic Tremors," *Newsweek*, Aug. 26, 1985.

4. *Citizen Action News*, Spring, 1985; Ilio Gauditz quoted in Phil Baker, "A Poisonous Plague," *Sojourners*, Nov., 1984.

5. *Newsweek*, Dec. 17, 1984.

6. *Ibid.*; Baker, "Poisonous Plague"; Samuel S. Epstein, Lester O. Brown, and Carl Pope, *Hazardous Waste in America* (San Francisco: Sierra Club Books, 1982).

7. *Newsweek*, Dec. 17, 1984; *Congress Watcher*, Feb.–March, 1985.

8. *Washington Post*, Feb. 14, 1985.

9. Cathy Hinds, quoted in the National Campaign Against Toxic Hazards brochure, 1984; *Portland Press Herald*, July 12, 1984; Caroline McCullough, *Indianapolis Star*, Sept. 14, 1984.

10. This and the following paragraph based on Boyte interviews with Al and Norine Danley, Feb. 26, 1983, Lowell, Mass.; Jean and Rita Pinard, Feb. 25, 1983, Lowell, Mass.; Phyllis Robey, Feb. 25, 1983, Lowell, Mass.

11. The report on Silresim is by J. F. Coburn et al., "Hazardous Waste Cleanup: Silresim Site in Lowell Massachusetts" (Bedford: Mitre Corp., 1979), conditions described pp. 2–4; state law described in Massachusetts State Legislature, "Acts and Resolves," chap. 407, p. 1; Boyte interview with Charlie Gargiulo, Feb. 24, 1983, Lowell, Mass.

12. Boyte Pinard interview.

13. This and the following four paragraphs based on interview with Esla Bynoe-Andriolo, Aug. 3, 1985, Chicago; newspaper stories from *The Dispatch*, July 2, July 27, 1985; Jersey City "PJP Landfill Task Force" memos, in authors' possessions; "Victory Against Toxics in New Jersey," *Citizen Action News*, Winter, 1984.

14. This and the following paragraph based on "1985 Superfund Reauthorization Campaign, *The Maine Alliance*, Winter, 1985.

15. Michael Wines, "Waste Dumps Untouched," *Los Angeles Times*, Sept. 7, 1984; Cass Peterson, "Superfund Record Challenged," *Washington Post*, Oct. 26, 1984; "Superfund Battle Heats Up," *Citizen Action News*, Summer, 1985.

16. *Charlotte Observer*, Sept. 18, 1984; *Chicago Tribune*, Sept. 28, 1985; *Lewiston Tribune*, Aug. 29, 1984; *St. Petersburg Times*, Oct. 15, 1984.

17. *Citizen Action News*, Winter, 1984; "Superfund-ing Battle Begins," *Citizen Action News*, Spring, 1985.

18. On Superdrive, see, for instance, *USA Today*, Sept. 6, 1985; *Philadelphia Inquirer*, Sept. 4, 1985; *San Francisco Chronicle*, Sept. 5, 1985; *Green Bay Press-Gazette*, Sept. 11, 1985; *New York Times*, Sept. 27, 1985; *Time*, Oct. 14, 1985.

19. Boyte interview with Mike Podhorzer, March 11, 1985, Washington, D.C.; *Time*, Oct. 14, 1985.

20. *Time*, Oct. 14, 1985.

CHAPTER SEVEN

Epigraph: "Grandma's Penny Sale," song by Larry Long.

1. Boyte interview with Anne Kanten, April 17, 1985, St. Paul, Minn.

2. Boyte interview with Joanne Klees and Marge Warthesen, June 29, 1985, Millville, Minn.; figures on farm income, *Minneapolis Tribune*, June 20, 1985.

3. Boyte interview with Eric Fure and Carolyn Slocum, June 29, 1985, Millville, Minn.; also Klees and Warthesen interview.

4. Suicide figures from *Minneapolis Tribune*, April 29, 1985; Kanten interview.

5. "Week in Review," *New York Times*, March 3, 1985; *U.S. News and World Report* special issue, March 11, 1985.

6. *U.S. News and World Report* special issue, for figures on debt; David Harrington, quoted in William Robbins, "Farm Experts See a Future of Fewer and Larger Tracts, *New York Times*, Feb. 17, 1985; "Middle Size Farms Endangered," *New York Times*, March 20, 1985.

7. Goldschmidt study described in Frances Moore Lappé and Joseph Collins, *Food First: Beyond the Myth of Scarcity* (New York: Ballantine, 1977), pp. 265–66.

8. *Ibid.*

9. John Lee quoted in *New York Times*, Feb. 17, 1985.

10. 1962 CED report detailed in Mark Ritchie, *The Loss of Our Family Farms: Inevitable Results or Conscious Policies?* (Minneapolis: Center for Rural Studies, 1979); see also League of Rural Voters slide show, "Minnesota's Stake in the 1985 Farm Bill," for a detailing of the conscious policies of corporate interests.

11. Story of "food power" in Lappé and Collins, *Food First*, pp. 256–64.

12. *Ibid.*, pp. 277–335.

13. Klees and Warthesen interview.

14. *World Hunger and the Demise of the Family Farm* (St. Paul, Minn.: Farm Organizing Resource Center, 1985), p. 3; Heather Ball and Leland Beatty, "Where Have All the Farmers Gone?," *Texas Humanist*, May–June, 1985, pp. 14–15; Jim Hightower, "The Reagan Administration's Cynical Response to the Farm Crisis," *Utne Reader*, Dec., 1984–Jan., 1985, pp. 88–91.

15. *Ibid.*, pp. 3–4.

16. Boyte interview with Becky Glass, Sept. 12, 1985, Minneapolis; overview of farm organizing also drawn from Becky Glass, *Farm Organizing Overview: Iowa, Kansas, Minnesota, Missouri, Nebraska, North Dakota, South Dakota, Wisconsin* (Minneapolis: Youth Project, 1985).

17. Stories on COACT organizing from *Minnesota COACT*, the newspaper, and Boyte interview with Joe Chrastil and Jeff Blodgett, March 18, 1985, St. Paul, Minn.

18. Chrastil and Blodgett interview; Fure and Slocum interview.

19. Fure and Slocum interview.

20. Description of farm bill from Hal Hamilton, "Barnyard Politics," mimeographed description in authors' possession; also "The Family Policy Reform Act of 1985," League of Rural Voters study, Minneapolis, 1985; Hightower, "Reagan Administration's Cynical Response," p. 89; COACT-Groundswell canvass described by George Knotek in Boyte interview, Oct. 6, 1985, St. Paul.

21. Merle Hansen, quoted in Hornstein, "Anti-Semitism," p. 4; Dan Levitas, quoted in CBS Morning News, Oct. 3, 1985; *New York Times*, Sept. 20, 1985.

22. Joe Chrastil, in Hornstein, "Anti-Semitism," p. 4; Boyte interview with Allan Libbra, Aug. 12, 1985, Collegeville, Minn.

CHAPTER EIGHT

1. Boyte interview with Lane Evans, Aug. 2, 1985, Chicago; David Moberg, "Populist Views Boost Liberals in Midwest," *In These Times*, Sept. 21, 1983, and "Evans Runs Again on Populist Agenda," *In These Times*, Oct. 17, 1984; Jerry Miller and Chuck Hudnall quoted in Moberg, "Evans Runs Again."

2. Evans interview.

3. Boyte interview with Carolyn Lucas, Sept. 18, 1985, Boston.

4. Richard Darman, "Historic Tax Reform: The Populist Correction," speech to the Institute for Research on the Economics of Taxation, April 15, 1985, Washington, D.C.

5. This and the following three paragraphs based on Lucas interview; Boyte interview with Miles Rapoport, Aug. 1, 1985, Chicago.

6. Boyte interview with Tom Hayden, Sept. 30, 1985, Santa Monica, Calif.

7. This and the following paragraph based on Boyte interview with Jay Westbrook, Aug. 3, 1985, Chicago; also *Cleveland Press*, July 29, 1977; "Muny Light Would Be 5th City Asset Gone," *Cleveland Plain Dealer*, Sept. 9, 1976; "Leaders of Council Are Among Seven Purged," *Cleveland Press*, Nov. 9, 1977; "City Council Gets a Facelift as Voters Revolt," *Cleveland Call and Post*, Nov. 12, 1977.

8. Boyte interview with Ira Arlook, Aug. 3, 1985, Chicago; story of Brush campaign drawn from Arlook speech, Oct. 5, 1985, Placid Harbor, Md.; also "OPIC Candidates Sweep to Stunning Victories," *Citizen Action News*, Winter, 1984.

9. John Herbers, "Grass Roots Groups Go National," *New York Times Magazine*, Sept. 4, 1983; Heather Booth, speech to Leadership Conference, Nov. 10, 1980, Cleveland; SLLP described and Tully quoted in *Citizen Action News*, Fall, 1982.

10. Interview with Michael Ansara, Sept. 18, 1985, Boston; Massachusetts Fair Share/Citizen Action, "To Protect Our Families, Neighborhoods, and Standards of Living," 1982, Boston.

11. Truman quoted in David Broder, April 29, 1984, *Minneapolis Tribune*; King quoted in William Robert Miller, "The Broadening Horizons," in C. Eric Lincoln, ed., *Martin Luther King, Jr.: A Profile* (New York: Hill and Wang, 1970), pp. 50–51.

12. Jack Newfield and Jeff Greenfield, *A Populist Manifesto: The Making of a New Majority* (New York: Warner, 1972), p. 10.

13. Jim Hightower quoted in Joe Holley, "Hightower Coasts to Victory," *In These Times*, May 12, 1982.

14. *Ibid.*

15. Joe Holley, "Hightower Plants Seeds," *In These Times*, Nov. 16, 1983; David Moberg, "Populist Harkin Battles Jepsen," *In These Times*, Oct. 24, 1985.

16. This and the following two paragraphs based on Boyte interview with Tom Harkin, Aug. 2, 1983, Chicago.

17. Congressional Populist Caucus, "Statement of Principles," 1983, revised 1985. The Caucus consists of the following members. From the House: Lane Evans (Ill.), chair; Jim Weaver (Ore.), vice-chair; Jim Bates (Calif.); Berkeley

Bedell (Iowa); Doug Bosco (Calif.); Barbara Boxer (Calif.); John Bryant (Tex.); Jim Cooper (Tenn.); Tom Daschle (S. Dak.); Byron Dorgan (N. Dak.); Charles Hayes (Ill.); Marcy Kaptur (Ohio); Bob Kastenmeier (Wis.); Bill Lipinski (Ill.); Frank McCloskey (Ind.); Barbara Mikulski (Md.); Jim Moody (Wis.); James Oberstar (Minn.); Tim Penny (Minn.); Bill Richardson (N. Mex.); Gerry Sikorski (Minn.); Mike Synar (Okla.); Harold Volkmer (Mo.); Al Wheat (Mo.); Robert Wise (W. Va.). From the Senate: Tom Harkin (Iowa), chair; Al Gore (Tenn.); Paul Simon (Ill.).

18. *Ibid.*

19. *Ibid.*; Velasquez quoted in Ronald Brownstein, "Great LEAP Forward," *National Journal*, Feb. 16, 1985.

20. Flynn quoted and LEAP history described in Bruce Shapiro, "Pushing the Progressive Candidate," *Fairpress*, July 3, 1985.

21. This and the following paragraph based on Boyte interview with Ladislaus Michalowski, Aug. 12, 1985, Collegeville, Minn.

22. Boyte interview with Doreen Del Bianco, Aug. 2, 1985, Chicago; also Hank Hoffman, "CCAG Triumphs in Hazardous Waste Campaign," *Citizen Action News*.

23. Penn PIC campaign described in *Citizen Action News*, Winter, 1984.

24. Boyte interview with Vince Hughes, Aug. 3, 1985, Chicago.

25. This and the following two paragraphs based on Boyte interview with Alma Hill, Aug. 3, 1985, Chicago.

26. This and the following two paragraphs based on Boyte interview with Gloria Fauss, Sept. 23, 1985, Columbus, Ohio.

27. Booth interview with Carol Browner, Feb. 11, 1986, Washington, D.C.

28. Boyte interview with Karen Scharf, Sept. 24, 1985, Albany, N.Y.

29. Harkin interview.

30. *Ibid.*

31. Boyte interview with Chuck Deppert, Aug. 3, 1985, Chicago.

CHAPTER NINE

Epigraph: Frederick Douglass quoted in "A Benefit for David Hunter, 1985," invitational card; Mercy Warren quoted in Mari Jo Buhle, *Women and American Socialism, 1870–1920* (Urbana: University of Illinois Press, 1981), p. 57.

1. Interview with Cora Tucker, March 12, 1985, Washington, D.C.

2. John Winthrop quoted in Richard Lingeman, *Small Town America* (Boston: Houghton Mifflin, 1980), p. 24.

3. Interview with Lynn Cardiff, Aug. 2, 1985, Chicago; interview with Alma Hill, Aug. 3, 1985, Chicago.

4. Herman Melville quoted in John Higham, *Strangers in the Land* (New

Brunswick, N.J.: Rutgers University Press, 1955), p. 37; Boyte interview with Tom Moogan, April 14, 1977, Brooklyn, N.Y.

5. For a useful discussion of the ways in which elite decision making is often concealed behind rhetoric of expertise and the free market, see, for instance, National Research Council, *Supporting Paper No. 7: Energy Choices in a Democratic Society* (Washington, D.C.: National Academy of Sciences, 1980), pp. 130–32; Booth interview with Alice Palmer, Sept. 3, 1985, Chicago.

6. Portsmouth quote from Raymond Williams, *Keywords: A Vocabulary of Culture and Society* (New York: Oxford University Press, 1976), p. 83; Mercy Warren quoted in Ted Howard et al., eds., *Voices of the American Revolution* (New York: Bantam, 1974), p. 135; George Warner quoted in Citizen Heritage Center staff, *Democratic Visions: Progressives and the American Heritage* (Minneapolis: Citizen Heritage Center, 1981), p. 14; see also Sheldon Wolin, "The People's Two Bodies," *Democracy* 1, no. 1 (Dec. 1980).

7. Hamilton quoted in Vernon Louis Parrington, *Main Currents in American Thought: An Interpretation of American Literature from the Beginnings to 1920* (New York: Harcourt, Brace and Co., 1927), Vol. 1, pp. 298, 302.

8. Industrialist quoted in *Democratic Visions*, p. 14; "To Win in Washington," *Fortune*, March 27, 1978.

9. Questions from National Conference of Catholic Bishops, *Pastoral Letter on Catholic Social Teaching and the U.S. Economy* (Washington, D.C.: National Conference, 1985), Jan., 1981, p. 38; commonwealth quote, p. 34.

10. Preamble from Richard Hofstadter, ed., *Great Issues in American History: From Reconstruction to the Present Day, 1864–69* (New York: Vintage, 1958), p. 147.

11. Between 1980 and 1984, the real disposable income of the poorest fifth of all families fell by 7.6 percent. For the second poorest fifth, income fell by 1.7 percent. The middle fifth saw a small gain, 0.9 percent. The next richest fifth got a larger income gain, 3.4 percent, and the richest fifth of all families gained 8.7 percent (John L. Palmer and Isabel V. Sawhill, eds., *The Reagan Record: An Assessment of America's Changing Domestic Priorities* [Urban Institute Study; Cambridge, Mass.: Ballinger, 1984]).

12. *New York Times*, Oct. 21, 1985.

13. Poverty figures from *New York Times*, Sept. 5, 1985; figures on portions of the population in poverty compiled from *Statistical Abstract of the United States, 1984* (Washington, D.C.: U.S. Government Printing Office); *Handbook of Labor Statistics*; U.S. Consumer Price Index.

14. On service sector employment and wages, see Ward Morehouse and David Dembo, *The Underbelly of the U.S. Economy: Joblessness and Pauperization of Work in America* (New York: Council on International and Public Affairs, 1985), Special Report 3, p. 14.

15. Corporate tax breaks under Reagan described in "Firms Raise Outlays," *Wall Street Journal*, June 6, 1984.

16. Report on high tech study from *Business Week*, March 11, 1985.

17. Figures on mergers from "What Mergers Are Doing to America," *U.S. News and World Report*, July 22, 1985; on destructive takeovers and speculation, see Leonard Silk, "The Peril Behind the Takeover Boom," *New York Times*, Dec. 29, 1985.

18. Korean wages discussed in *New York Times*, Feb. 20, 1986.

19. Interviews with Lane Evans and Tom Harkin, Aug. 2, 1983, Chicago.

20. Boyte interview with Sonia Hernandez, July 5, 1983, San Antonio.

21. On these themes, see, for instance, National Research Council, *Supporting Paper No. 7*, chap. 6; Paul Goodman, *Communitas* (New York: Vintage, 1960); W. W. Harman, *An Incomplete Guide to the Future* (Stanford: Stanford Alumni Association, 1976); E. F. Schumacher, *Small Is Beautiful* (New York: Harper & Row, 1973).

22. Thomas Jefferson quoted in Parrington, *Main Currents*, p. 347.

23. For elaboration on these themes, see National Research Council, *Supporting Paper No. 7*.

INDEX